Identity, Trauma and Existentialism

Developed - 2023-2024

Published by McWest & Associates
ISBN - 978-1-971928-08-1

New York, NY
United States of America

Identity, Trauma and Existentialism

Baruch Menache

Table of Contents

The Dichotomy of the Existential Character

We continuously reside in existential pandemonium, although we alleviate its burden of emotional attribute using several methods. We make use of identity, family, relationships, security, and philosophy to temperate the burden of existing in the overwhelming dark matter. Identity informs an individual as being part of a specific culture and no other, becoming a familial organization that provides conceptual depth and personal intimacy. Familial, as the word suggests, is to establish certain individuals as familiar to exist in an intimate setting while discounting all supplementary beings. Security is the provision of a safe habitation, preventing the notion of trespassing the realms of abnormal and unknown. Philosophy and its intellectual counterparts serve to convey to the psyche on concentrating on a specific pattern of thought; hence, the term 'discipline' is appropriate when describing all intellectual categories. To surmise: family represents all social relationships, security characterizes the private-ness of a domain, identity embodies a sample of all social cultures, and discipline is the dosage of conceivable thoughts. These local services are mitigated by existential formalization through a systematic structure.

These shall be discussed in the succeeding chapters.

Let's begin with the familybody, simultaneously containing inborn existential mayhem that presupposes its fortification in addition to an external existential realm which offers protection from it. The inborn existential manifestation can be found in the form of the bond between children and parents. The familybody is an exhibition of a parent's experience of nonexistence which has been submissively accepted through happenstances. The offspring's attempt or assumption that the experienced presence of their existence is expected from their parents creates a problematic love-bond from the onset.

Another aspect is the inability of a safety-net to replace the existential burden alongside the incapacity and inability to appropriately attend to child rearing. One is tasked to construct a higher life form, something that another peculiar higher life form will lack the ability to understand, surely to implement. Thus, the child is prodded into a setting in which they will be dissatisfied, carrying a reservoir of unfulfilled necessities. However, with all of that said, the family asserts the privilege of being a habitat of existential safety, which is to succeed in that regard, not to shy away. Moreover, the wording of 'safety' is technically incorrect, as for a familybody to engender a domain of complete safety would be contrary to the reality at large and would not be an accurate representation of it.

A public family, or one which has more to gain or lose in the communal sphere, will always be recognized to provide an accurate portrayal of the existential familybody. Each aspect of their lives is cherished and pronounced in the public domain; a domain that is assumed to be the arbitrator of absoluteness for reality. Thereby, the underlying hostility which is brewing within a familial structure has a chance to see the light of day, as those details are considered worthy of attention. Each member will be in their respective standing, as would seem archenemies, which is only a pronouncement of the proceedings within each familybody. Elevated amounts of jealousy, contempt, resentment, and the like will manifest only for the reason that the communal body has dictated this particular familybody to be recognized in all its amounting.

The case of two children: one who has gained social status while the other who has not, were already in a hostile environment at the beginning stages of animation. Each had sought to be the superior parent's offspring, by being a numerical value of two it would appear that the other is illegitimate. Each would seek to prove their legitimacy, and the veritable child proceeds to demonstrate their appropriation of the superior parent as an imperative to proceed in their intrinsic existence. However, preceding these events is the problematic proclamation of each offspring to their innate existence, which only upon the pondering of the superior parent begins to seem doubtful. Such that in a child's privilege for the superior parent's lineage, they are in pursuit of a more secure existence for themselves, something which the superior parent cannot provide even if they willed it so.

The representation of a single child for public validation will demarcate a final outcome of the situation and resolve the child as the legitimate one. Thereby, instead of it being a lifespan conflict, with each gaining a certain stride or presumed advantage to prove their legitimacy, the case has already been unraveled. The second child must admit the role of illegitimate child and remain in the subservient backdrop of a certain proclamation of nonexistence. The only method to gain a sense of existence is to recognize the matter of existence itself. That conflict between children is only a representation of a former hostility to which each higher life form is chanced with. In that, we are residing in a balance of, on one side the proclamation of nonexistence portrayed in a transient life, and existence in the sense of veritable presence of the moment.

The children are not privy to such complex analysis and their instinctual mode of analysis is to assume the superior parent to be the complete mode of existence and with them being a continuation of that. If absoluteness is within the superior parent, then only an exclusive continuation of a single likeness would be considered existentially compatible and not simply a resemblance. Thus, it becomes irrationally assumed that the rest of the siblings are illegitimate.

It remains to be seen in what way this is possible since one child seems to exist in the presence of the other and must be sourced from somewhere. The siblings are not declaring that one of them did not succeed from the superior parent, but rather that it was a roundabout or insincere blunder that slipped from outside the realistic state of affairs. They are compelled to admit that the superior parent is lacking absoluteness, although it is assumed to be a minor deficiency which offers the availability for a notion of illegitimacy to be its resultant. This is not a recognition that existence is not in the hands of the superior parent, instead it is to admit that they are not the complete picture of reality, with a seeming broader framework which surrounds them. Thus, the illegitimate argument is born from a recognition of the broadness of the world which encompasses the superior parent. However, there is no conclusion that the superior parent is themselves of partially nonexistent material, and so we can have siblings assume one another to be illegitimate.

Once the siblings mature, they can recognize that not only is the horizon more comprehensive and the superior parent more liminal, but existence itself is a questionable item in both the superior parent and in every aspect of nature. The feud of siblings begins to seem both illegitimate and illogical, although remaining a potent impetus throughout the becoming of the individual; seeming as this was a part of their formation, and such material does not get removed from the arrangement. Furthermore, there is a certain legitimacy to the initial argument with a certain method of reflection.

The superior parent comprises the potential of the child, so that even as we have settled the existence debacle, the child assumes that it can only expand in proportion to the potentiality of the superior parent. When there are two children, it would seem that the potentiality must be partitioned. When a child seeks to expand beyond the allocated or presumed portion, they begin to gross from the portion of the other child. Thus, hostility is renewed with the success of a sibling, who seemingly has taken stock from the other's territory.

Upon introspection we can learn that the potentiality of the superior parent is assured with the potential of their corresponding superior parent. Then we must scale this perspective and acknowledge that all of humanity is part of a single source of potentiality. The allocation of potentiality from the modest superior parent becomes an inaccurate account of the situation. Within the superior parent's structure encompasses the potentiality of the single primary source of nature, for if they have derived from that substance then they surely enclose those elements. Still, we must demarcate a boundary between superior parent and their derivative parent, to which one must complete the encasement of potentiality with the superior parent before deploying to the grand-superior parent. The ability to perform a cross-boundary incursion is granted when all the succeeding potentially has been exhausted. If they were to exhaust the complete reservoir of the superior parent, even as the expansion is beyond the superior parent's potentiality, the children will accordingly be in opposition.

Besides this analysis which diminishes the potential of the children's feud, we can acknowledge that these are all conceptualizations, albeit major in its formation and more intimate than any other, yet still remain an intellectual analysis of a string of events. Taking account of the wholeness of reality we can discount both legitimacy and potentiality as constructs, to which any human can be whatever and however they would like to be, although such conceptualizations remain in the foreground of individual existential makeup and cannot be dismissed. Thus, when jealousy and levels of hostility rise, we can acknowledge where they are existentially sourced, even as we consequently dictate that one must develop their moral grounds in response to the traits of jealousy, hatred, resentment, and others.

We must account for the biological or in other terms, absoluteness, of the children's patterns of thought, to which their respective conceptualizations, albeit in a certain respect have merit, require a more comprehensive analysis. This would be the potency of semen emitting from the progenitor, which in a reductionist view contains the material of all the subsequent events proceeding it, to which the child and all subsequent activity will be generated. While each child contains a lineage to a specific parameter of semen, they depart the reduction of their intrinsic makeup and begin to question their validity in the prospect of the other sibling.

The child externalized towards the situation of another child and they re-internalized that information to contrast the innate nature of their respective semen. This moment of externalization transformed the process of thought. The apprehension towards the sibling began from an interest in the surrounding environment. The child offers the reflection which initiates the feud, but hitherto was only a proponent of an environment for which the other child was pursuing. When the environment proved to be different than the inborn recognition of selfhood, it placed a wedge between siblings.

However, it is not the presence of the sibling that proves contrary to subjective reality, but rather the entire environment, far beyond the present family structure. Thus, the feud of siblings in its adulted form, where one proves to be the fruitful one, is a manifestation of a preceding frame. The efficacious child characterizes the wholesome environment to be a member of social achievement, while the other senses their inadequacy in the appearance of that environment, validating the sibling's posture against their innate biological reality. This is on the subject of the community's recognition and that is the real aspect of the feud owing to the subjectivity of each child exemplifying themselves as determined by the environment. Success will be of interest because the environment is emphasized; an environment which contradicts innate selfhood and estimates itself as a comprehensive reality and arbitrator of the concept of success.

The resolution for the sibling who has socially exceeded the sibling pool is to alleviate the burden of these authoritative conceptualizations that will certainly manifest. This is accomplished by conveying the familybody into their respective dominion, as the child has taken the role of superior parenthood for whatever social cause, such that the familybody requires consequential superior parenting from the sibling member under social transcendence.

If we were to analyze the situation correctly, the prosperous child, notwithstanding, is involved in that infantile conceptualization of illegitimacy and potentiality. The only change is that this member has taken the role of absolute legitimacy and potentiality. This habituates the familybody in the resentful dissemination of potentiality from this member and their respective social environment. This event is no different than the child beckoning for the potential of the superior parent. Especially if the members surrounding them are with a stressed claim to their legitimacy and potentiality. The potentiality registers in the hands of that sibling and the other members will be unable to access their potential without first encompassing all amassed potentiality of the superior child/new parent. Since this comely outcome does not prove to be forthcoming, the next point of conjecture is to imagine as if they were accessing a higher degree of social transcendence. A worse outcome would lead to the case of hostile jealousy and maybe an attempt at pleasing the potential by conceptual force or violent choices.

Instead, the ultimate outcome is the family members' transition to the new superior parent which initiates a superior parent-child dynamic with them. They can then access a partiality of the new superior parent once again and thus the process reoccurs in its complete cycle. However, this is not a usual transition because it would require a certain admission of disappointment in the initial stage of birth, to which they have spoiled their access to the original superior parent.

Once such a level of humility is accessed, the members can now assume the process over again, for which they can gain a reservoir of advancement, albeit on the shoulder of the superior child, but enough for personal progress of a life cycle. Towards a juncture when this reservoir is exhausted and another member will be available by taking the mantle, although as a sincere process. Otherwise, it will be reimagined with underlying hostility throughout the transition and will be ousting the potential to assume the prerogative of potentiality; an epoch of stagnation.

Existential Safety

When identity, familybody, physical security, relationships and other foremost themes of philosophy fail, it accumulates a cosmic interference of the masked existential commotion. This can be appreciated by negating the impression which has been dutifully imprinted upon the psyche; a swift absence of devotion to create a highly exposed state of selfhood. For the child, this thread is most discernible as they are predisposed to these structures of existential comfort and have acquired no skill in mastering or even experiencing such a state. Second to that, the natural state, into which a human is born, is a state of loneliness towards the eventual procedures for that existential buffer; we could acknowledge the sentiment, "an individual is born alone and dies alone," to equivocate the existential disorganization of the parent and child despite the supposed familybody to which a child is born into.

We are naturally presupposed to the experience of the forsaken child, which was not the commonly attributed cause of faultiness on the part of the caregivers but a negligence to protect the child from their inborn nature. The causation is more accurate when attributed to the failure of uncultivated systems that wouldn't soften the natural state of existence.

This state of existence, as nature had set forward, is the state in which one experiences its most downtrodden and vulnerable features. This is due to the deep-rooted state of existence which does not appreciate its innate existence, although maintains enough cognition to recognize such, catapulting the human to the extrinsic realm for the search of external formalizations which will provide counteraction to that proposition. While having no anchor at which to settle, the natural state takes over, manifestly as existential mayhem and its associated symptoms. The neglect of the caregiver fails to anchor the child into a calm state, neutral if you like, in the waters of existence and there is no alleviation from the overload of nothingness. Thus, love is not the natural response from nature but a remedy to its empty forces. *Love is the blind passion which gives respite to existential chaos.*

An enslaved individual has acclimated to a constitution and formation that is devoid of identity; a family within a jurisdiction, insubstantial relationships, security for the organism, and philosophy for their characteristic initiation. The conscripter maintains the role of the enslaved individual's entire existence, all their systemic structures far beyond the notion of identity and rather exemplifies the child-parent dynamic. They can only think and act in a manner to which the handler would think and act, being dependent on them with every element of their understanding. When the enslaved individual is suddenly granted access to all those aspects which were prior dependencies, especially without the tools of a mature citizen, they plunge into an experience of existential mayhem. This applies with a degree of slighter measure in the occasion of a servant or worker.

This transpires in a similar function for one to gain independence from a dominant culture's dynamism which preserves a widespread influence upon the psyche. Independence is met with a plummet into the cultured state which survived outside of that influence, generally far less established. The cascade is owed to having a prolific culture to be a structural dependent, which upon release causes one to immediately pursue a cultural outline of any variety. For instance, an indigenous population commences towards a centric culture to be quite enamored at the meta-data of sophistication which is at their disposal. However, further into this process can possibly endure a degraded degree of attachment to it, with an immediate requirement for an alternative framework; to which their former existence proves promising.

The conflict is that even as an enslaved individual, the dominant culture had a certain influence on their character, one which does not depart during the period of freedom. Thus, the sediment of the prominent culture remains, whilst the realistic state of the enslavement becomes exposed. This contradiction has the effect of providing an understanding that is merited enough to utilize certain surface material, but short of developing and expanding itself.

If we are to understand this criterion of being short enough, we must approach the psychology of the affair. For the example above, the ensuing culture is applied to particular zones of selfhood of the newcomer, in that they contain a certain context from the prior culture to perceive the advanced one. Specifically, by default of being a diminished cultural outline serves the notion that it is void of a proper orientation to reality, for it is swept away in the face of the evolved culture.

The transition between the two has the individual seek the aspects of the previous mindset within the new territory. For there is no culture which cannot be relative to deficit aspects of contemporary orientation, and would be the periphery of the existing culture's dynamism. Thus, the indigenous individual benefits from the culture, nevertheless will be a mockup portion contrasted with the aspects that are relatable to known self-perception and does not prove to be the principal theme from an objective standpoint. Enough it will be, because it does provide a heightened sense of whatever is being sought and serves as a better practice for being associated to a welling center. We would acknowledge that, of the same character, being a margin enclosed by an oppressive principal theme is superior then being the chief theme of a non-principal order.

The availability to expend the dominant culture will be in standing of the culture of enslavement. This will initiate them to maintain the position of the conscripter, in the effect of its existential freedom, whilst being the identity of a slave in their outlook of the edifice. The enslaved who has the supremacy of the conductor is a critical weight, since their accurate description is an enslaved individual with the authority of action as the presumed agent. They grasp subservience and dependency to a very fine scale, allowing their supremacy of action to be the context of those traits. However, those traits, when propelled into the public light, causes trouble to every level of its organization.

Demanding subservience and dependency will suppress all creative talent and peculiar characteristics of each of the participating members. The authentic role to statesmanship is to assist aptitude towards its potentiality throughout the many components of the state; something that cannot be absorbed with a lack of training. Coupled by the notion that owed to their acute development of the opposing traits of subservience and dependency, it would require a counter-measure of equal or more acuteness to have them relinquish those elements. This is only one of the many difficulties which can occur with such a transition.

A subjective analysis of an individual who is both enslaved and the presumed agent, would have their activity allied with ample confidence while still understanding very little of the intellectual web behind the action. The level of their cultural aptitude at the present moment is one which does not comprehend higher meditations of action. For an organization or structure to run smoothly, actions must correspond to its associated comprehension, and when contrary, every action will constitute a disappointment before it initiates.

For instance, one who impersonates a doctor, by not obeying that level of essential education will execute in a critical manner with momentary satisfactory results. The subjective experience which does not parallel the action with coinciding aptitude, characterizes the situation by a sequence of unfavorable decisions, each leading to further negative consequences, all without a comprehension to effectively address the challenges. Doctoring actions without cognition is brutal, overtly intimate, and predatory to the vulnerability of mortality.

Take the case of the disingenuous doctor, while the patient receives sufficient healing for the moment, the doctor will assume a higher degree of aptitude which will open the door for more doctoring. Eventually, this will lead to the case of medical administration which will prove catastrophic. On the side of the patient, initially receiving adequate treatment, may return to the doctor, entrusting to provide proven results. There could be a circumstance for which it does not lead to any matters that can constitute a problem, however, the innate experience of utilizing actions that do not align with cognitive apprehension will demarcate a separation for future activity to be allowed a severer detachment from cognition.

We may think that the bondaged-one permanently resides in existential turmoil due to the natural diminishment of all of these structures, e.g. identity, family. Since social beings are unable to continuously subsist to an overwhelming experience, they will attach to whatsoever to liberate themselves from that disorder. The enslaved, first and foremost, existentially fastens to the presumed agency, becoming vehemently attached to the extent that their subjective experience is synonymous with the agency.

The conscripter's identity, familybodies, relationships, security, and philosophy are entwined with the enslaved sense of existence. When freedom transpires, the conscripter's influence decreases with an outstanding existential dark matter for them to contend. In fact, we could make the argument (we have responded such queries in another portion of this work) that it is forbidding to place enslaved individuals at liberty since they will deal a tremendous burden, one which they don't have the tools to handle. Differing from the conscripter who arranges the dark matter from time to time and has an array of methods to handle such an experience. The enslaved is without that, having barely a worthwhile existential experience since their imposed drudgery did not allow for such amenities.

Birth is the same character, since the involvement of a literal birth is joined with existential commotion associated with the birthing parent's pain and uncertainty, while on the other side is the child's proclamation of life. The moment of birth, when the child's head crowns till its feet are loose, is the quintessential moment of both the chaos of existence and the assertion of life: scaling that encounter is the umbilical cord, either the attachment to the oblivion within birthing parent, thus, the possibly of non-existence, or the detachment in the direction of complete mobility and individuality.

The enslaved, to access freedom, would require an inner resource that is counterintuitive to the corresponding state of being. Since servitude itself had occupied the entirety of personhood, to reach beyond that would require a surge beyond rationality. Seeking sincere recognition of the material within the existential fissure that is evidently concealed is found to be wearisome, while rationality can be promptly articulated.

From a virginally rational perspective, there is no logical aim to disrupt the natural occurrences of life. A narrative that is not based on the present moment is not a realm which can be considered superior or more utilitarian. This is quite accurate and rational, a free individual in an existential frenzy must confront a more treacherous life than a vassal who does not tackle that emotional commotion. Even if we were to voice the enslaved individual to how extraordinary it is to experience a higher gradation of autonomy, it would be like trying to convince the birthing parent that the chaotic affair is beneficial for sustained life. For the victim, as for the drudged one, such a conception runs counter to the whole essence that is possible from the experience. *They would necessitate reaching beyond what the mind can comprehend to sequence the mind to expand its unique comprehension.* The psyche does not expand outwards from an internal epicenter but rather expands by negating itself and aligning with substance beyond its natural inclination. Later, there is the attempt to make sense of that disparity with the prior centered locale, although futile for a full reconciliation.

The experience in the present moment contains a limitation and its development can only ensue linearly. The experience can be understood in a variety of dimensions, ensuring that it uses the experience itself to question its innate nature. For instance, the birthing person has their entire state of personhood participating and the development of that experience is related to its nature. They can take note of the subtleties in regard to their perception, memories, associations, relationships, and intricacies of thought. The limitation of this process is that by fastening to the state of experience, they cannot make use of all possible knowledge which may assist in a higher degree of development.

This can be done by reaching beyond the experience, which will neglect the present moment and its contents but will uphold access to all knowledge, such that it would not result from an unadulterated effort upon experience. Thereby, they can seek out a higher narrative which illustrates the emergence of animation, or the dimensions of change that will ascend from this new birth. The experience of new life is not the natural experience, yet it can highlight the details of that pain through philosophical introspection. The new dimensions that will ascend will not be a part of the natural experience of birthood; ideas which cannot relate to the current state of existence, or in other words, the mere internality of mind.

In fact, of all our experiences, there will be an element which is accessed from an external locale of that experience, with language itself being a component of an internal dialogue which has the requirement of initially being communicated. Experience itself never needs to be thought in order for it to be realized. Outside knowledge will always be necessary if one desires to develop an experience. The thrall, by reaching out into the abyss of the unknown and its knowledge, can now bring such material back to their fundamental experiences for subsequent development. Therefore, the mere act of letting go of an experience and seeking knowledge that is not directly linked to the experience is an act of existential acuteness.

This is less seeming with a free citizen because they can seek knowledge beyond familiarity and not be uneasy about the existential surge. They have many measures to assist in alleviating that burden in order to explore to a risking depth, having welfare methods at every corner. The concern of shelter against existential chaos is that the knowledge that is being sought may not be a resultant to be brought back to natural experience. There is no incentive for levitating the natural state of existence since existence itself has been insured by many measures.

We may wonder as to why such a citizen would seek knowledge and existential risk during the initial stage, having found such safety in their own existence. Despite all the safety measures, the existential chaos makes itself known at intervals in a citizen's lifespan. This can be noted by such occupation axioms, "I knew this is what I must do," which situates to a period of existential chaos which commanded knowledge. The fact that this piece of knowledge should be fixated indicates to the immediate reassertion of those safety measures. Thereby, the knowledge will be solely focused to combat or divulge that memory of existential unrest, while never being used to develop one's universal experience since the safety measures are standing upright. Thus, we arrive at the individual who shadows specific fragments of knowledge without integrating that knowledge into overall experience. Especially disconcerting in that the existential experience is the cause for one to initially seek out knowledge, having the hope that it will make a homecoming to raise the entire state of the psyche.

A parable—

A parent who has all the comely children at home and finds the experience to be enlightening. One day, a dispute arises between two siblings, a dispute which continues for days without any resolve. Troubled by such an interruption in the harmonious atmosphere of the household, the parent seeks a solution. There was much contemplation in regard to the state of affairs, understanding that the solution is not available within the family and only outside its doorways will they find help. They scheme a plan, in which the two siblings will be sent to different neighboring farms and will work in their new environments. The idea was such that each sibling will enter a new environment of learning which will assist to enlighten the homebody after a certain period of time. Implementing the plan, each departs the household with a heavy heart and an adventurous spirit. The siblings are both fruitful in their new environments, having made a name for themselves as being industrious and well-adjusted. The parent, having learned of their success, had sought them for their return. However, the siblings, having forgotten their petty sibling rivalry and the troubles of the homebody, had them enthused to progress in a direction that was farther away from the family. Thus, they began to think of a future far beyond the state of their particular family. Desiring to establish their own enterprises with all the knowledge and experience they have gained, they decide to form a partnership and depart to a more prosperous locale. Before departing, they are resolved to return to their parent to bid farewell, as the likelihood of returning was nil. Arriving at the doorstep of their former home, they embraced their parent for that tearful separation. The parent thought, they were sent for the purpose of gaining a greater good on the outside, away from those tumultuous times. Yet, instead of returning with the newfound wisdom to sustain the harmony of the household, they join forces to abandon that domain.

The cause for the siblings departure from the homebody is that they find the familial space inadequately shielding against the existential chaos, and secondly, a discernment of the homebody's inherent institutional shortcomings. The homebody, if performed in a proper manner, should not be the perfect shield for existential disarray, since the child must find that disarray and explore their own secluded sense. As a response, the child will initially reach into the abyss of that existential chaos and create their own formulation of that existential substance. Concurrently, they will take a path of reconstructing the institution of the homebody, motivated by the failed attempts of their caretakers.

The very failure of the established homebody inadvertently gives rise to the very existential chaos it sought to shield against. Consequently, the child is cognizant of the duality of the homebody; its protective elements and its letdown at providing protection. This dual awareness becomes the impetus for constructing a new home, one that rectifies the existential vulnerabilities of their upbringing. The hope of the new home is that it builds a safety measure which was ineffective in their own upbringing. Even as they are motivated by their parents' failed attempt, they will use that model in building their respective home. This is due to the fact that the parents had been partially successful in sheltering them from existential chaos.

When the child believes their parents' home did not have existential leaks or that whatever the homebody was, it did not assist in shielding them from the existential chaos, they will miscarry in their own pursuit of that. The former will be excessively devoted to their parents' home, never departing from the confines of that homebody even as they may be substantially accomplished. The latter will not make use of the factual aspects of their inborn childhood which did assist in their existential disarray; this in turn will cause their new homebody to destablelize with ineffective existential reasons for its animation. The impetus for constructing a homebody is due to a personal settlement between partial success and partial failure of their caregiver's homebody. There would be no purpose to construct a homebody if one conceives that their innate rearing was a complete miscarriage.

We may postulate that one can be motivated by the social environments which will assist in the deficiency of familial functionality for existential disarray. However, such models won't justly have one engaging in the undertaking as it would be existentially situated. The social class does not esteem the existential regard of the familial because of various biological factors. The only manner of probability external to the familybody is the endeavored construction of a new familybody. Furthermore, the mere quality that one opts to construct a new homebody is a statement to society that their rearing homebody was partially fruitful. Even with all the refutations and postulations, the actuality of the situation is such that all new homebodies are built as improved versions of previous homebodies.

Disciplines

Proceeding formal education in specific disciplines, individuals may grapple with a myriad of potential thoughts and their sense of selfhood. There is no filter for one to sift the ingress of information in a competent and productive manner. Higher life forms can opt for the psyche to labor on autopilot, which is the most natural usage of the organism. While if they choose to utilize their psyche, essentially taking over nature's role, they might initiate a process of thought material which leads to existential material that readily can be the onset of psychosis. Therefore, even before the instant of conceptual freedom, a necessary discipline must be in effect. This will allow the psyche to be narrowed and distilled into sub-domains which can maneuver the flow and flourish with its influence.

Rituals are the preliminary structure of a discipline because they provide the activity that goes alongside the conceptual framework. For example, circumcision dating from the Egyptian dynasty, provides an intellectual discipline to make use of existential disarray in the form of a conceptualization concerning a specific activity. The ritual afforded an activity in the supreme personal aspect of personhood with its impactful results, forging as a discipline for greater cognitive and communal recognition.

To illustrate, we can demonstrate the conceptual implications which are the primary aspect of this ritual. Sexuality is an expression of the most intimate aspects of a higher-life-form structure and the associated region takes part in that conceptualization. There are various portions to the organ and the component selected for this activity is the protection of the organ. With an analysis we can formalize the embedded conceptualization, indeed, removing the concealment of the most intimate part denotes to the psyche that intimacy must be revealed. The secreted version of the organ would have one presume (notably after circumcision has had a cultural influence), that it remains secure as an intimate component and cannot or should not be unrestricted.

The act of industrializing the organ as a communal domain would seem to initiate an impartiality towards intimacy. However, contrary to that, the organ can now articulate its intimacy without being sheltered. The sanction of something intimate to be enclosed and protected is a core basis for an absence of intimacy. The rationale of the philosophical clause is that deficient intimacy deprives the passion for animated life form, while diluted intimacy is always available for restructuring.

To illustrate, a romantic relationship will always consist of two individuals who are justly integrating into society and consequently finding intimacy from that. Each partner consists of a fulfilled existence and through the acquaint interactions they passage into a place of intimacy. We cannot imagine a scenario where two partners were mandated into a dynamic that brought forth authentic intimacy. The prospect of intimacy must be conveyed through exchange, once external entities slowly recede into the private setting for actualization. The intuitive doctrine: the sexual organ should be 'open' to societal interactions and with all ensuing considerations, should find a collection of intimacy to express one's innate desire concerning all those interactions. When the organ does not nude itself to society and correspondingly attempts intimacy, it cannot access an authentic version of it. Intimacy is a direct affiliation with that which is not intimate. When the relationship with non-intimacy disengages, a coinciding diminishment of the degree of intimacy incurs. One can only be private if they engage with the public, otherwise, they are not undergoing a private state.

The forfeiture of foreskin is to bank on a positive sexual behavior that will prime to an intimate experience. This does create a conundrum, since the exposure might go to an extreme, in which all publicized sexual behavior dilutes intimacy. Hitherto, the forfeiture indicates that it would be a worthwhile conceptualization, as *an absence of intimacy is regarded far worse than diluted intimacy.*

Such is the philosophical view which can be pronounced from a domain which is assisting in the existential commotion. In this instance, it is an identity-related ritual that is performed in that narrow arena of identity-related components of personhood.

An instance of a discipline that parallels identity is the homebody. It behaves as a narrow interplay of complex information, which to perform its duty forthright, shall be explored beyond the mere safe connotation. In essence, we are to explore the domain of existential protection and gradually proceed towards risk-management in the existential aspects that can be safely uncovered. Each layer is to be paralleled in line with the existential aptitude of the individual, so that the child will approach the family in a rather ironic form, while the mature individual will enter into communion with these constructs with an availability to expand its existential limits. At a certain juncture, the mature adult reaches a stage for which the systemic aspects of the familybody are not necessary and only its silhouette is necessary to proceed towards an array of further inquiry.

Intellectual pursuits are only as good as they reach a locality of intimacy. The most prolific scientist who cannot incorporate their discipline into the confines of intimate relationships does not obtain existential resolve. They enter domains of outstanding intellect but cannot make use of it for the activity of what is familial. The mathematician may fail to bring numerical mysticism into the discourse with intimate relationships. Thus, for the transition to occur in a manner which encompasses existential disarray, the intellectual layer must encounter those intimate relationships.

Like the aforementioned, the ritual is an act in which everyone partakes in. As the chaos of existence takes hold of the mature adults, they begin to unpack the activity into various disciplines. Since an activity may constitute a ritual, a discipline can be derived from it; in the aforementioned example, becoming a study of sexuality. Throughout one's engagement of a developing culture's system, they are encouraged to further the discipline however they deem appropriate.

This is not to discourage intellectual disciplines that are not associated with a developing culture's rituals. As a society develops, certain disciplines arise which are the manifestations of new perspectives to tackle the peculiar existential disarray. An identity can be loosely connected to every discipline in terms of their own ritualistic activity. They can identify the discipline of physics to be aligned with the study of nature, which can surely bridge to any identity. This may or may not handle the existential disarray according to the ability to bring such information into social activity.

The solution to a newfound culture is to maintain certain rituals for which the competent adult will find respite from existential disarray; more fittingly, will be a mechanism for safely engaging with it, whilst learning in a distinctive domain and available for the horizon of possibilities. The progression of civilizations would no doubt offer new disciplines which are distant from any dynamic relationship with a pre-existing culture and its rituals. Therefore, new rituals will requisite to be added, especially pertaining to the new disciplines that are relevant for a progressive spectrum of ideas.

Another method for such a dilemma is that the members of the new society would maintain two identities, one for the new system and a second for the pre-existing culture with its rituals and disciplines. The concern arrives when the newfound culture consists of rituals, which, if they do not adhere to the activity will not obtain existential respite from the discipline. While, if the newfound culture were to follow the universally influenced rituals with outright adherence, they can easily neglect their own, since existential calm is seductive. The solution would be to engage in the progressive culture's rituals, but, with some reservation. This reservation is to sanction and empower their respective rituals to be commandeering in consequence that will never threaten its base.

Dialogue between Cultures

The contemporary equivalent of a ritual can be found at the foundational layer of psychology, therapeutic practice. This ritual entails two or more individuals to engage in dialogue with one another. They assemble in an enclosed dynamic, unrestricted from interferences, while each proponent is dutifully committed to guaranteeing the conversation remains realized through its allocated duration. Each participant is partaking in this ritual by allowing the natural rules of social relations to fade, exploring portions of individuality in a manner that even an intimate relationship won't necessarily award.

This becomes a ritual by its non-normative structure, so as to obtain a conscious conceptualization of something peculiar to its actions. The objective of the therapeutic conversation is not for the relationship that may manifest from such an interaction, thus, contradicting the existing actions. Though, it has the alternative objective for which the entire therapeutic tradition is concerned. The procedure itself is ritualistic and it would be disconcerting to reenact it outside the given clinical parameters. This ritual allows for the temporal engagement of deep intimacy, which is precluded in standard sociality for suitable explanations. We can say that this ritual is defined as: a controlled dialogue which explores every subtle experience of personhood, free from the normal reciprocal exchange of dynamics.

Therefore, one who participates in traditional rituals may be reluctant to share in the newly founded ritual, and indeed, will never find respite from the capacity of the discipline of psychology, that is, until they enact a true engagement with this ritual. The study of psychology imparts an impressive amount of our present-day familiarity through its impact on society. Without this ritual in place, we remain informed but not engaged.

Devoid of adhering to a contemporary ritual such as this one, an individual will invoke a state of existential commotion as the information resides on the top of the psyche, while the remainder of the psyche is not in agreement, connection, or discussion. Information is transmitted in various ways and might appear without a certain deliberation to its contents or even a recognition of what they are. Without adhering to the general themes of the embedded society, it will be the cause of this floating layer that is incapable of being settled.

To admonish the ritual would disregard the political establishment which consists of its natural contemporary rituals. Understandably, some will not be privy to the structural information behind the ritual and may assume it to be inconsequential. We may not know the material depth of a ritual to justify a disengagement, yet, we are still partaking in that society's exposure. This would immediately invoke a detriment to the psyche, causing a form of discontent to arise. In the therapeutic example, when discounting the ritual practice, there will be information that will make its way to the conceptual domain. The moral and philosophical implications within the discipline will be a steady influence within that society. Hitherto, the primary ritual which can deal, understand, handle, incorporate, and discuss the information-material is not being retrieved.

Each identity may have their unique opposition to a ritual, whereas this example is a demanding ritual so that the subsequent identities must concede to its prominence. Essentially, one is engaging in a ritual that may be peripheral to personal identity. Hence, we can find problematic derivatives, where one would affirm the effectiveness of the therapeutic ritual in contradiction to their identity's rituals. To an extent that even a representative of an identity may assert "therapy comes first," utilizing the clinical aspect which is estimable of utmost deference. To be consistent with our terminology it would be, "to manage the existential disarray, the genre of psychoanalysis is to be more consecrated of an approach and effective in its final outcome."

Through a synthetization of the therapy ritual and traditionalist culture it may promise the continuity of both realms. Most identities already contain conversational rituals, and to tangle the two would not be so challenging. Apparently, this seems quite simple; affix a contemporary ritual to an array of prevailing rituals. When such a synthesis takes effect, the psychology discipline begins to superintend all the existential effects or benefits of the other identities. What transpires is that a single contemporary discipline can restructure an entire identity.

Therefore, to successfully manage this conflict, it would be incumbent to not incorporate the therapeutic ritual into an existing identity, but rather to treat it as an external ritual of another identity, or in other words, deferring to its classification as that of the developing or pre-existing culture. This will consent to approach the ritual with some reservation. As psychology is embedded into the fabric of contemporary society, this would be an archetypal subject in which attention would be required.

This process can be found during the initiation of any major identity, in which there is a great concern for not superseding the existing culture. This can be viewed as a well-designed approach for any new culture while engaging with its pre-existing culture. To thoroughly accomplish this, first, maintaining continuous dialogue between the two cultures, as decorated with representatives of each. Second, through the dialogue, the participating cultures do not become a synthesis to culminate into a single grand culture. Third, through the dialogue, the resolution is not to arrive at a perfect consensus and rather that each perspective is made transparent for each side to acknowledge. Fourth, throughout the dialogue one should engage behind the position of their respective culture with stronger vigor than the opposing culture. Since the purpose of the dialogue is to understand the opposing side while still maintaining one's particular position, one must place a tenure of existential vitality within their respective culture. Fifth, the culmination of the dialogue is realized when each culture embodies the role of the opposing culture, to which the lines are slightly blurred between the representatives.

Essentially, the resolve is to encompass as much of the other while still maintaining a distinct separation. If there is an absence of dialogue between the less and more dominant, or if there is a preoccupation for which two distinct identities cannot be made out, then the reciprocity has failed. The former is true because the dominant culture will overhaul without the indispensable conversation, by virtue of its prevailing dominance. The latter is true since the dialogue causes a single side of the dynamic to reduce their own role for the sake of conversation or participation. What seems like a learning experience, in which one side succumbs to the other, is essentially the negation of an individual's substance of learning.

When an individual seeks to choose a more dominant culture than their respective background, it must always maintain discourse with the developing one. However, since the rules of dialogue do not allow one to completely synthesize, instead, the dialogue should assist in understanding everything from the vantage point of the opposing culture without negating the preceding culture. Then, with all of that information, one could further the initial identity with an enriched form. There would be no scenario where one could step away from the initial culture and take upon themselves a more dominant culture. In such a circumstance, they would be attempting to neglect the pre-existing culture while subconsciously incorporating the entirety as a mechanism to orient into the new culture.

This is problematic considering that culture and identity are an amenity to deal with existential disarray. When there is a mesh of differing identities and cultures, there is no temporal location where it conducts the full scope of existential layers. The quality of existential service is that it must be able to access wholeness of personhood. Thereby, one would depreciate into an existential crisis until a distinct identity can be secured from the combination. This identity must be singularly paralleled to one's personal cultural commencement; albeit available for enhancement through dialogue with other cultures.

Once the dialogue transpires, the representee could return to their role as leader of the newfound identity along with the pre-existing traditions and its intellectual material, while the pre-existing representee can retort with a satisfaction of the status quo. Any further attempt at dialogue would be to neglect the purpose of the dialogue, succumbing to utopian farsightedness, having the innovative culture convey the entirety of the pre-existing culture to be triggering their modified version of it. If the representatives sought a complete synthesis between the two cultures, they would have betrayed the purpose for arriving at the dialogue in the first place; representing a particular culture.

Unfortunately, the dialogue may reach a point of tension which is reduced to violence and war, all to demonstrate the potency of each argument. It becomes a form of virtuosity, in which the physical prowess is shown to stimulate the swing of the pendulum to their distinct side of the conversation. If the pre-existing culture asserts a notion of the argument, the counter activity of violence will be nearby to be displayed in contradiction to that assertion. This, we have come to know as political violence, which are direct acts of violence for the sole purpose of demonstrating a side of an argument.

The interesting point of consideration is that the representatives of the pre-existing culture are in agreement that one should master all of the existential disarray, which is the basis for all identities and cultures. However, the pre-existing culture falls short by insisting on a proposition which does not include certain aspects of the existential system, the product of which is a fallout for the encompassing society. It seems that the representatives assume that such underprivileged components of the system do not contend with existential disarray. Although it remains problematic, for whatever components are part of this system, they are in affiliation with these neglected components, demanding of them to integrate into the inclusive undertaking of its culture. Therefore, it would seem that the fallout is due to contestation on the grounds of relationships, in how one must seclude themselves from parts of the system despite the detrimental effects.

Another point of contention is that during a prior juncture the pre-existing culture was in their infantile stage. They would be effectively discounting their own creation-story as inconsequential for contemporary life, akin to a twosome neglecting their anniversary or vital romantic memory. Thereby, alluding to the fact that those memories are not necessary for progressing in the current environment. The pre-existing culture does not regard that connection to be consequential, even if there are noticeable connections between the creation-story and its manifestation in contemporary life. This pattern of thinking is owed to a lack of symmetry between the contents of the culture, making it difficult to adjoin the memories together.

First, we must link all the dynamism of the biosphere to a distinct source before we can conjure memory and history to be relevant in the present moment. Each strand of experience is interlinked to which the formulations of present day are a product of our history. The pre-existing culture may oppose such a notion, whilst gradually demonstrating that primarily — it is the irrelevant memorial content of the infantile stage that presides over the conversation. This can go to such an extent that by the culmination of the dialogue, they can become wholly irrational like that of a child.

We find this sentiment preceding the final moment of transition away from the pre-existing culture to which the representative of the developing culture espouses sentimental anger towards the pre-existing culture. The beforesaid is a response to the pre-existing culture's crude, artless, and unrefined manner of halting the discourse midway. The developing culture harbors resentment towards the pre-existing for forsaking the role in the dialogue, despite having the representative of the developing culture assume a stand-in role for the pre-existing culture. The discourse of any discussion should be dynamic oriented and surely this particular dialogue with its immediate implications concerning the depth of reality.

Normal dialogue would have the participating members resolved by entering into the confines of their opposition, which would have them understand the opponents' point of view as their own. When this is not the impetus of the conversation, both would submit to feeling neglected and unfulfilled, having to assume the role of a proponent while the counterpart remains in their initial position devoid of any existential risk. The neglected proponent will be assuming the new role and its perspective, although benefits their personal learning, will be an existential fissure.

A complete exposure of one's vulnerability would be departing one's preserved post, and accordingly, removes the existential cushion that has them enjoy an assumed understanding of existence. The discourse requires that each proponent departs from a certain bliss of existential comfort, which would be at the advantage of integrating into a higher state of existence through the dynamic. There are three points of alteration through the dialogue: the departure of selfhood, the ingress into an alternative individual framework, the return to selfhood with both perspectives intact and distinct.

The departure of selfhood would always be chanced with an existential experience and would remain as such even with the integration of an opposing perspective. The return to selfhood is the only state that would exhibit the opportunity to find respite from the unsettling state of existence. When the proponent does not perform this ceremony and adheres to the starting position, it causes the other proponent to be consigned to continuous existential disarray. They cannot return to selfhood because the other proponent has not held the position available for functional repositioning.

The departure of selfhood is a complete process which includes a true negation of one's proprietary propositions. The reason that one is willing to perform such a deed with its subsequent risk is that the proponent will be entrusted to collect their initial position and have it bookmarked until there is a dynamic return. Each proponent is occupied on behalf of the other to ensure that their initial positions exist at the point of closure, culminating at the end of the dialogue. The term 'seeking closure' becomes appreciated, having one proponent neglecting to reciprocate the initial position of the other; now lost to them. Neglect can be the cause of both types of proponents, one who does not aspire to revisit a prior version of themselves, or the other, indisposed to offer the former version to the one missing it. The latter case can transpire because they are disappointed to receive the position competently, or they may have forgotten its substance.

We are reminded of highly intelligent people who engage with the downtrodden of the populace, placing themselves in a precarious position. The disparity between parties causes the incompetent individuals to fail in comprehending the original position of the other. When the moment of consolidation arrives, intelligent individuals are at a loss between two perspectives.

The developing culture is recognized at the culmination of the dialogue, while the pre-existing culture never departed from its position; avoiding absolute integration into the developing culture's manner of life. While the developing culture had wholeheartedly entered into the pre-existing culture's role, which had them existentially distressed by the fact that the pre-existing culture does not retain their initial position. This prompted the developing culture with resentment, which had the pre-existing culture remain silent in their admission of culpability.

Consequently, it is the resentment at the culmination of the dialogue which denotes this. The pre-existing culture continued the initial position of the developing culture, which was due lost to the developing culture's diligence in supporting the dialogue. They may explicitly assert this, "You are not wanted," while the developing culture may retort, "I am still here." The pre-existing culture situates that they had exposed themselves with complete vulnerability, positioned for the dialogue. The pre-existing culture is making a claim that they have gone even further than the developing culture, for which there is no reason for the developing culture to remain in conversation. As if they superseded the developing culture in the positioning of their proponents and there is no need for the developing culture to partake in any further discussion.

The pre-existing culture retains the initial position of the developing culture, and the developing culture does not contain a lost position of the pre-existing culture; they have never departed from their initial stance. The culmination of their lack of harmony would demonstrate that the pre-existing culture is the one who has not completed the dialogue, and therefore, with much devastation, coercion, and conviction, must continue the dialogue with the developing culture.

When there is no specific identity that pertains to a culture, individuals may adopt multiple identities and cultures, causing confusion as to where they stand in the conversation. The objective of two individuals relating to one another is that each offer what the other does not have. When there is widespread agreement on everything, the relationship develops to be unrelatable. The remaining connection is rather two distinct individuals that are fused together. Even within the rumination of one's psyche, when there's agreement on patterns of thought, the psyche-material blends together and breaks down. We may think of fusion as a superior notion but in essence it is a form of disintegration. When two aspects do not have any distinct characteristics they become one, and when the unified entity does not interact with opposing aspects then it condenses onto itself. An individual who engenders neutrality in thought patterns will begin to degrade and lose apprehension of complexities and self-awareness.

Producing an aspect to be relevant is that it opposes another aspect, thereby, value can be attributed as an external factor. All forms of learning are of the same theme as one must be in opposition to the material as this will foster the material its ability to teach. If one amalgamates themselves with the material, then there is no objective for continued interaction as the material appears adequate on its own. The material can only engage with an individual through an embodiment of an opposing character and all material competes with whatever one may presuppose.

The astute individual will find the areas of contention and enact an internal argument against it, while the misguided individual will find areas of agreement to find validity to their perspectives. This validation is causing them to become estranged from the knowledge itself as the material already agrees with them. This estrangement will cause one to further pursue a grasp upon the deteriorating knowledge which will only make them prideful of the information.

Pride is the declaration of knowledge for specific material all the while losing comprehension of that information. This is the reason that the trait of pride is necessary for such an individual. The pre-existing culture can be seen as such a figure, commencing the dialogue with a blanket axiomatic statement which embraces all necessary components and has all vulnerabilities patterned. The profound wisdom it would take to know every aspect of the current situation, let alone to discount the prospect of new information, demonstrates the estrangement from their database. Moreover, there is a sentiment of pride in the statement; its function, to embrace that current position while internally degrading.

The disappointment emanating from the pre-existing culture has all their counterparts interrelating with substance that will only contract what was already understood. The lack of opposing characters within their subjective perspective causes them to mislay their knowledge. This always comprises with a natural disregard for children and their caretakers, with a weighty dismissal of their part in intellectual development, which if they were, would have been an opposing character by virtue of their needs, innocence, and intuition.

Like all despots, they begin to lose their complexity by the circumstance of being surrounded by agreeable sociality. Therefore, by virtue of the developing culture taking a mere stand as an opposing character was already the beginning of an accurate learning experience for the pre-existing culture. Based on its foundation in consequence of the failed reciprocity of the pre-existing culture, we may approximate that the developing culture would retain axioms and traditions for the purpose of maintaining opposing discourse. This would be enacted with a mandate of various varieties that children and their caretakers become a part of the communal discourse, which by virtue of innocence will always be an opposing character. Hence, the developing culture engages with substandard individuals, to serve as an opposition to their enormity. Among the top tier of the communal body, they would be encouraged to maintain opposition and thus innovation.

We find the manner in which the developing culture transitions from the pre-existing one will determine the future developments. By following the most treacherous path, exposing themselves to their past, the security pillow will be lifted, for the objective of progressing in an arena that is solely theirs.

Had they scampered into a new domain, they would have erected insecure thoughts regarding their culture and that which was left behind, unable to initiate something new. Whilst in the culture, they had not stepped away from that arena, so that a confrontation would not remove the pre-existing culture's claim. Also, the transition must occur in a state of existential uncertainty to advantage comprehensive security and its associated safe place.

The same occurs with various disciplines for when over-stimulated can hinder dynamic patterns of thought. The specific science is a dosage from the pool of all intellect. When that discipline becomes over-disciplined, there is a lack of interaction with other psyche rumination and in effect becomes disconnected from social reality. We notice certain sciences retain peculiar linguistic forms, which may be no different than a tribe in seclusion. This has been the situation in regard to the research that led to the recent pandemic; a discipline which did not interact with sociality. Had they taken a perspective of a selection of the masses in their view of such lab activity, they would have immediately disrupted the research, no matter the benefits. Notice that the ascetics of contemporary lab activity is overtly isolationist for it does not interact with sociality even as the tradition of science does. This was a strain that the pre-existing culture endured, although intelligent, had dealt with the known disciplines with too much passion.

A central theme of a developing culture is the need for sensitivity toward the subcategories of a social system. We find a microscopic approach to every detail in the eventful disambiguation of a sub-social society from its overarching benefactors. A volatile motion in any direction would cause this sub-social environment to either: become self-possessed, delineating the source of universal information and movement, or become inattentive to the changing environment of a new movement and social system. Both can produce devastating results, for the movement that becomes detached from its embodied universal culture will lose its vitality as an organized structure, increasingly becoming dependent on the universal system.

Contrary to the belief of a developing movement which presumes that being detached makes them self-sufficient, it is only in the case where there wasn't a previous duty of dependence on the structural elements of that culture. However, being that the movement is a derivative of a larger movement, namely the pre-existing cultural system, it will be dependent whether its members agree to the proposition or not.

We always find this in nature, when a dependency is not appreciated to eventually envelop the system. A child who is adamant about their self-sufficiency by assuming their progenitors and childhood caregivers are non-essential facets will create an environment with the complete dominance of those internalized figures. The reason for such a reversal is that a failure to attend to the source of one's subjective or biological experience will cause that information to seep into everything. The material will enter by any means into one's domain, just as the memorable notion of the pre-existing culture and its universal representation will always enter into the sub-society with more veracity, being of a preceding and more universal perception. That information which is already a fabric of the sub-society will make itself known, akin to the repressed information making its way to the conscious psyche through various means, even against the active choice of the individual.

Homebody

Family can isolate itself from the collective by overstimulating those familial relationships, in that the family is separating from broader social interaction. The stranger, in reference to the family can be perceived as either sharing in the collective group from which the family originates, or as something intrinsically foreign. When viewed as the former, the notion of the stranger has the continuous potential to become part of the familial structure. With the latter, the stranger is foreign and is not considered as a possibility. The familybody which views the stranger as completely foreign, also assesses its internal members as such. By defining the non-familial parts of the collective as foreign, they are defining the entire collective, a direct derivative, as foreign as well. What allows it to be a relationship is that each member is separate nevertheless still engaging. When all members become interconnected by discounting outside relationships, they cease to be connected in a relationship manner. The family evolves through an initial process of interacting with the collective to then home in on a particular being or set of beings to be constituted as private. When a private group of people disremember their original outline they become secluded from it.

One's private abode has a clause which demands to partake in another abode if lacking the necessary sociality to make for a habitat of sophistication. Even as the private home is a safe place, away from the overwhelming collective, when the homebody is absent of relationship material it would be necessary to group as a collective. The defining factor of assembling the homebody as a habitual space is its degree of attachment to the collective.

There are two distinct nouns to apply here, the 'home' and the 'group'. The home is a privatization of the collective, though contradicts the notion, being attached to the collective while still departing from it. The group is the bridge which facilitates these two contradictory facets, in being neither the home nor the collective. The habitable homebody that includes the stranger does not negate its private status. When the stranger becomes a portion of the family, the unit performs as a group, consisting of familial members and collective conjunctions. Thus, the stranger is a representative of the ambiguous familial relationship with the collective and becomes the bridge which allows the family to exist. To style a proper abode, one would need to ensure the connection to the collective remains a priority and the stranger becomes essential to the homebody space.

The monster is both beast and higher life form, the demon is both angel and higher life form, the zombie is both psychotic and sane, and the ghost is both inexistent and existent; each wedged between two realities. Therefore, there is freight in relation to them, because one who doesn't reside anywhere also resides nowhere. With this reasoning, strangers and their connective tissue to the collective can be the governing nature that will upend the familybody. Alternatively, if we are to incorporate the stranger to ensure connective tissue to its thematic element, we should also include the monster, demon, zombie, and ghost.

First, we must understand why the incorporation of these amorphic figures is so important to a developing culture or correspondingly to a familybody. Amorphic figures naturally oppose classical states and they serve to be an opposing character. This in itself will assist in highlighting the existential dialogue that any monster will bring up. The monster questions the status quo of being, in their state, and in their existence. Therefore, the monster ensures that one will never have the outcome of the pre-existing culture since it always obliges the pre-existing culture to face their existence.

The second article that amorphic figures bring, in this case to a homebody but correspondingly to a cultural institution, is the realization that there is more potential that is not being harnessed. The mere stance of an outsider under the auspices of the homebody cultivates a reverberating sentiment that they are entrenched in a settled identity and not utilizing all possibilities. This will compel the familybody into that specific dialogue. The monster, on the other hand, represents all the repressed animalistic states that one could get wind of.

Allowing all animalistic states to be expressed is not part of a developing culture doctrine, while the homebody, on the other hand; an essential component. The demon represents the existential potential which failed through its developmental phase, retelling of all existential matter that hadn't made it to actuality. The zombie, being that psychosis is more prevalent, is something an individual may benefit a perspective. The ghost represents what is concealed and is not favored in a developing cultural tradition since the material that is exposed will be mistreated or overstimulated.

The underprivileged individual is also an amorphic caricature since they do not reside in the classical state of sustenance. They represent the existential ability of currency through its various usages, hence the motif of the affluent individual finding disfavor with the underprivileged. The affluent comprise the depiction of the potential and the underprivileged represent the possible avenues for which the affluent may be bothered by existential enquiries. Yet, a progressive individual is to incorporate the underprivileged since it will offer a constant reminder of a better procedure of their currency; assisting the underprivileged will contrast one's presumed necessities. The deprived individual represents the potential of currency and will contradict that premise with an act of giving and retract the potency of currency. The interaction has the recipient surpassing one's innate needs, just as the stranger can disintegrate the homebody. An individual who does not have those necessities doesn't requisite the potential of money, just as one who is homeless does not need to recognize the potential of housing. Both are in constant exchange about what is needed and therefore do not require external lessons. We might find an altruistic motive where one should assist even as it doesn't offer dynamic exchange, yet the assistance will cause moral detriment and the choice shall be measured accordingly.

We may find that various amorphic characteristics are incorporated into a single entity, the poor individual may be homeless and the stranger may also be contracting psychosis. Therefore, incorporating an individual in the midst of multiple amorphic traits may include aspects which are not necessarily recommended. The psychosis feature would enquire the mental state of all the family members, which even as may be effective through a research endeavor or religious duty, it will shape and alter the rest of the homebody towards the psychotic state.

The homeless individual, although emphasizing adequate enquiries about the potential of the homebody, also causes the entire homebody to degrade to the stature of the homeless individual. The incorporation of the stranger or homeless individual must be restricted so as to not break down the privatization of the homebody. This would defeat the initial resolution of incorporating the stranger. The stranger is to offer the homebody a reminder of its potential and if they cause the obtained stature to degrade, it becomes a problem. According to the development of the homebody is the degree to which they can handle the incorporation of the stranger. A measure should be had, so that the stranger imparts to the family for self-consciousness, which in turn tolerates more strangeness from both individuals and multiplicity within the familial structure.

A familybody comes to mind, who nursed vagrant folk and had them snooze in their lounge and others would dine regularly. This is an example of a maximum development of the familybody, with an eventual capacity to incorporate all these radical interactions without neglecting their possessive structure. The same applies to the clinician who navigates the complexity of psychologically related circumstances, gradually allowing additional capacity to incorporate these mental states, all the while maintaining their personal sanity and competence. This is endured through context, for instance, to be able to impart psychoanalytical theories.

Without the broader social intention, which this problematic social dynamic is in service, the relationship concludes with two proponents of equal standing. The psychotic states of the individual would become more organized, and the clinician to be more psychotic. Indeed, the patient is only an opportunity to the later conversation of esteemed guests in their journey of higher learning, to which each interaction with the patient is, "I must discuss this interaction or idea." When such context is not part of the interaction, although the patient will gain greater advancement through reciprocal transference, it will be at the cost of every subsequent patient.

If a progressive doctrine is to shape a community and regimen that is opposed to the pre-existing culture's erroneousness, the foreigner becomes the solution. Had the pre-existing culture incorporated the foreigner into the private domain, institution, or state, this tyrannical development could never have occurred. The pre-existing culture would have been already branded to discount the foreigner and would not take kindly to immigrating notions. They would have rituals that would serve to discount the inclusion of the foreigner, such that it may be a wonder as to how a new culture could ascend with innovation at its side.

When the pre-existing culture lacked an array of astute individuals to adequately assess problematic situations, they would necessarily seek out the foreigner. The non-citizen would transport the opposing intellect, one which is required for continuance, being as they lack internal diversity. This may be a way to incorrectly deduce that economic gains prove a steadfast culture, whilst it was the external faction that had caused them to flourish, both intellectually and economically. However, when practiced for an extended period, which should have led to higher degrees of rationality and the recognition of universal unity, it was found to be exasperating. The external faction becomes a sore sight, being a reminder of dependency for their developments. They would vigorously have them demoted by deliberately discounting the backbone of their culture and placed at the barest end of the class spectrum, avoiding their presence and the ensuing dynamic offering. In essence, internally degrading to such a point that they are resistant to disclose that an unknown had instigated all their accomplishments.

During dialogue with the developing culture, the pre-existing culture exemplified all this, with the developing culture proving that their intellectual abilities were in a vertical decline. This is quite a reminder to a new culture to avoid such a mishap by means of adhering to their internal memory, especially infantile stages. Which is also the manner in which one will be able to connect to the general thematic element of culture, since external factions remind one of their intimate influences, especially one's infancy.

The Child

There is a single child in every homebody who represents the continuation of superior parenthood and urgently swarms the superior parent for the progressive path to which the evolution of the homebody would prove efficacious. This child can be termed as the potential of the homebody and will display the raw movements toward progressive change, or in certain situations to identify the incompleteness. This child will usually retain a masculine tendency to embody a sense of potential that is presiding in the existing situation, while the feminine tendency will present potentiality in the universal sense. The former methodology will tend to the structure of the homebody as it is, while the latter form will tend to the universal realm in reference to the disparity between society and the homebody and thus, a form of potentiality as well.

In terms of proper attunement, while the universal reality is equitably a pathway for a homebody to embark on, the certainty of its existing situation is imperative since it follows a logical sequence of that distinct domain. With the universal sense attended, it will disrupt the current situation and will neglect the logical coherence between the homebody and the universal reality. With a process of success, a coherent universal structure will overhaul the entire homebody, disregarding the homebody as a distinctive seclusion. Sooner or later the realistic necessities and intentions of the homebody will seek to be expressed; although against a very commanding current of universality to which it won't be a prospect. Instead, the very present individualism within the family structure will be repressed and become the haunting motivation to all one's universal stipulations. Thereby, utilizing the universal sense will cause one's personal realm to lay dormant and may be infantile in nature, having not a moment of interaction or development.

This is not an argument towards the necessity of the existing situation against the universal sense, as they are both pertinent to a cumbersome individual and homebody. Rather the expression of its existing structure and its particular potential is the core of the homebody, while the expression that tends towards the universal sense deserves its proper domain. A homebody that is devoid of the universal sense can still be considered a homebody, although without existing apportioning becomes removed from the equation.

When we encounter a homebody that lacks the universal sense, we find a great number of assumed realities with varying components that are not derivatives from a genuine locale or center. The structure may be attempted with integrity and will coincide with an integral form, nonetheless, uninformed of the reality structure which outlines all these perspectives, like a child demanding change without knowing the realistic outcome that they are requesting. As mature individuals, we can dissect the situation to identify the needs and requirements of the child that are unbeknownst to them. They will not depart from a certain parameter of inquiry, to which we can always find the realistic material from the situation; however, they diverge from the true conversation for one that is simulated. For instance, a child might disrupt adults of a given scenario with specific intrusions that prove to be exactly what mature individuals happen to fear. The child intuitively identifies the vulnerabilities and thus exploits them to the detriment of the adult. However, the child is not seeking to disrupt the flow of maturity but to make aware their flaws so that both adult and child enjoy a sense of progression and validation within a dynamic setting.

The child may approach the scenario by means of simulation, by the order to attach to the surrounding maturity by intruding on their vulnerabilities. A singular scenario which most children understand is one of conflict since that is one-dimensional. The child cannot understand that they represent the vulnerabilities of maturity as to assist the progression of the homebody or institution. This is something that a deliberate education will bring, with the onset of maturity having these ideas incorporated. Thus, the educational layer allows for a more direct analysis of the situation and accordingly, the child is directed to a more coherent approach of the situation.

We can acknowledge that a lack of universal sense to which we can analyze the scenario and are given a default setting of conflict for which we cannot process the situation in terms of its genuine intentions. However, we remain with a simulated version of a personal scenario of the homebody, and this can be considered adequate in terms of a foundation for the homebody.

This fluctuates when the above example is missing from the equation and the child is assumed to be erratic toward an undefined aim, while the adult is frustrated being disrupted from their specific objective of the moment. Thus, we will envision two distinct individuals who have differentiating aims that happen to intersect in a conflicting manner. This will remove the entire homebody from the balance and each proponent will tend to their aim despite the intense emotion which happens to arise in this situation.

The adult may seek a further progression of their aim so as not to be disturbed or will place prevention methods so as to deny access to the child to be able to intersect again. The child on the other hand, may assume a certain inability of the determinate adult and will further their aims towards other more receptive adults. When the situation proves to be the equivalent for all maturity that surrounds the child, they will attempt intrusions upon society as they are appear as a single unit of erratic and inconsequential aims; they being the matter of consequence as the offspring of that realm. The child may question their own sanity as it appears that their intuitive sense is not to be agreed upon by anybody of maturity. What is also occurring is that upon the non-responsive situation, they assume the homebody not to exist and their entire existence resting upon the homebody to be questioned.

The foundation of the homebody also correlates to the initial stages of the homebody which consists of a primary child who is consciously or otherwise prepared to represent the existing structure in its progressiveness and vulnerabilities. When the primary child who is representing the structure becomes a topic of contention then we identify a trend where the homebody is restructuring. Indeed, we can acknowledge that the homebody is disintegrating into the universal sense to which they are slowly granting more territory. The final situation is that the homebody will lose its structure as they become a group of individuals with universal aims that chance to reside in the same locale. However, this will not outlast the situation and the vulnerabilities that lay dormant, and merely trivial contention will dismember the unit for each individual to begin the progress undeterred in their universal aim.

The primary child usually takes this role because all the other siblings are in some effect participating in this choir. The primary child leads by the biological priority and every proceeding child will produce certain remnants of the primary child instead of simply reverting to the parents. Those who are naturally inclined to the universal sense will not participate in the equation and only will do so in providing an educational privilege on their assumed reality. They are the messengers from society within the family domain, while those who represent the existing situation are the foundation of the familybody.

The parents are not considered the homebody in this context as they are so embedded in the existing structure that they don't have the entitlement. Only other biological entities which endure that chain can present themselves as the potential future. The child represents a quantity of the homebody but does not inherently retain that substance for themselves. Even as the child is a reminder of the parents' vulnerabilities, they are not innately within that state.

In their respective psyche, they are an existing structure that continues to be parental figures of their own. When they display the vulnerabilities of the existing structure, they are attending to their existential demands about their distinctive nature. The surrounding environment is only a landscape for the child to unleash their inquiries. This continues throughout the child's life and the parents are the first individuals to interact with their dispositions. The child may have certain unmet needs; however, it is not the parents to which the child is most unsatisfied, but their inborn existential nature of having so many prerequisites. Also, with the needs unfulfilled, it is only upon the competent mature individual whom they are wary about, as they appear to have the ability to fulfill their needs and still do not do so. This is upon all of society since it is not only their immediate surroundings that have failed to provide, but all capable sociality.

We can prove such a theory by attending to the mindset of the infant at the parent's behest. They do not think that the breast is specifically of a singular connection while there is a broader world with more aspects. Instead, the breast is the sum of reality and the non-breast aspects are existential chaos. This never changes, for we are always viewing the known aspects as the entirety of reality and the unknown as existential disarray. The view of the child towards the parents is only an example of universality, and when the purview widens, their respective parents are demoted to an iota of universality. We can argue that there is a very pronounced bond between individuals and their parents. This is only a reflection of an infantile perspective when the parents were considered universal, and since it was embedded in their psyche it is quite difficult to reflect on the conception; a universal assumption and not a private one.

We have established that the child is not fundamentally the potential of the homebody, nor the representee of the homebody. Neither is the parents the true formula of intimacy, as they are a universal sense that the child assumes until their horizon broadens. Yet, the child represents something pertinent for the homebody, and this is what we are in discussion about. The child has the ability to represent something while not being the existent substrate of that representation. They are not chosen to represent and are rather naturally formulated due to the degree of shared intimacy which was experienced. When the child experiences a situation as deeply intimate, they begin to embody the persona of the proponents of intimacy.

The child carries an embodied version of the surrounding situation and then deals with that information flow. When they come upon a disparity, they reach back to those individuals for questioning. The child is not fundamentally the embodied version of anybody, and thus the question of a seeming vulnerability is not genuine. Therefore, we depict the scenario as a representation of an individual who only embodies an externality to thus represent it.

The child represents the vulnerabilities of the homebody because they have downloaded the parents' persona and identified the disparities and inconsistencies. The reason we can trust the child for such an ability is that in their attempt to incorporate the personas, they experience an inability for attachment, and it is those areas that are most troublesome in the homebody structure. Similar to taking apart a structure to be moved to another location, what will derive from the process is the vulnerabilities of that structure, some to be discarded, some to be restructured, and others to be questioned and discussed.

The child is following such a process, and even with a low level of intelligence can identify all the varying mistakes, as they are earnest to partake in the entire persona. The primary child will embody the parents with such veracity that they will contain all the information to extract for the progression of the homebody. The rest of the children will embody the primary child in their embodiment of parents and will represent the vulnerabilities of the homebody as seen from the vantage point of the primary child.

The difference is that each proceeding child will only embody a certain aspect of the primary child, and when spread out, each will represent a piece of the primary child, while the first will represent the entirety of the parents. There will be those children that do not embody the parents or the children, but rather the universal attachment in respect to the parents or children. They do not care for the genuine character of the parents or children, but the process of attachment from parents or siblings onwards. Universal attachment is more important, so that when maturity takes hold they will immediately attend to broader universality. They do not completely detach from the prior engagements because they were the ones who announced their attainment in attaching to universality. They will naturally perceive the homebody as a way to further their external attachments and they are disinterested in present intimacy within the archaic familial structure.

For a society which has its individuals attend to the universal sense would be like a child who attends to familial attachments to absorb the notion of general attachments. When much of society is in such a configuration, we can be sure of two things, one, there is high achievement and progression rates, and two, the primary child is the most contentious subject. The primary child which embodies the parents and represents their vulnerabilities with the associated potential are not an appreciated conversation. Firstly, they represent the deficiency of the present homebody, pronouncing an immediate distress.

Secondly, for those of the homebody who are further interested in the universal sense will maintain an existential margin for the multitudes with aspects that are neglected for the universal aim. For them, the primary child will be the representation of existential chaos itself and will be repressed as a subject. Interestingly, the components of the homebody representing the existing structure will be able to handle the primary child as the postured representation which at its most detriment state is considered a decadent homebody. However, for the constituents that allocate for the realm of universality, the primary child is assumed to be the murkiness of the night and will be avoided both in physical and mental form.

Let us now discuss the troubled scenario which has the homebody adhere to the primary child and a framework that methods the vulnerabilities and potential of the homebody. There will be a sense of a homebody in such a situation; however, it will denounce the children who attend to the attachment itself and will take upon themselves the universal system. Those children will be considered outcasts and when present in conversation the entire aura will placate them with possible disdain. They will be debarred from the intimate interactions of the familial structure, and whatever activity to prove otherwise is only an attempt to provide a certain civility for familial hegemony.

The vulnerabilities that arise from the primary child will be dealt immediately so as not to insist that something lies deeper than the assumed situation. When there is trivial conflict, each will placate the other until there is a sense of forgiveness and satisfaction. There are no questions as to why certain contention arises, as the assumed direction is immediate reconciliation. The conflict is thus short and the process of reconciliation even shorter, which has the entire episode as a non-learning entity, even as this is what the contention intended.

Another possibility is that there is a high degree of manipulation and flattery towards the primary child, whatever contention arises, it would seem uncomely to have it manifest in the social sphere. Extra devotion is awarded which would seem to provide worthy relationship material but is a process to calm the spirit so as not to arrive at any vulnerabilities. This is like dealing with a resentful contrarian by providing so much excess that whatever mode of behavior calls for sincere resentment becomes a notion of imprudence. The hope is that the primary child will remain a child for all of life, so as not to attend to the mature conversation and the instability of the current system.

The child that one begets is the representation of the vulnerabilities and potentiality of themselves. Indeed, the child also represents the existing system which displays a fixed scenario for the consideration of the parents. However, the parents are not fixed objects and can alter the immobile system in any direction. When change occurs, the child will retrieve that shift and display another version of vulnerabilities and potentialities for further examination.

The parents are placed in a difficulty as they are constituents of another family dynamic and produce their representation of vulnerabilities and potentiality of their respective parents. They cannot attend irrespective of the prior system as they are caught between two realms. If they were to follow the representation of the child, they would further the existing system; although without deliberation to the system that they came from. In this respect they would prospect even as they isolate themselves from the source of that progress. The child only acknowledges the mishaps and the possible horizon of the existing system in terms of their respective needs. This will not highlight major vulnerabilities which are not seen but are in effect, nonetheless.

For instance, if parents concentrate on related aspects, the child will highlight such in effect to decry those vulnerabilities and posture conceivable growth. However, the parents only deal with these issues due to certain experiences during their childhood. This is owed to their parents experiencing episodes which may justify that outcome. This may seem like unserviceable information to the child, one that does not need to be deemed a priority. The parents are required to interact with their historical environment which brought such addendums. This is to avoid further experiences of such a situation, which if the perspective of the child is all to account for, will not be entertained. Although the child should be taught the possibility of environments that produce such calamities as to attend to such mishaps;

nevertheless, it will not be a part of their interaction.

Yet, we still recognize the representation of the child to be more relevant than the position of the caregivers in respect to their former families. The parents were carried through that environment as newborns and allocated growth with an extensive duration of coming-of-age. These developments had brought modification to the parents for which they had become an entirely new enterprise. At the stage of begetting the child, the representation that the child evokes is far more accurate to the caregiver's current situation. Even as the caregivers evolve, this is done alongside the particular development of the child for which the information will remain current and precise, until that is, the child departs from that circumstance. The position of the caregivers in their former families is dated and does not account for the individual change which accrued in anticipation for maturity. At most, it can be reviewed in hindsight for aspects that may or may not be relevant. The parents cannot re-occupy with their former familybody to permit certain relevant material to take effect since the act of maturity was a defiant moment in which they had initiated to formulate a new system.

This process cannot be reverted since each instant that passed through the gates of maturity is contrary to such an activity. When the current familybody attempts to integrate with their former bodies it will revert every mature process and begin to date everyone to childhood or nonexistence in reference to the children. The other approach is for the current familybody to interact in the context of self-exploration to which those de-dynamical bodies are mere avatars of historical precedent. The relationship is arranged in reference to these contexts and will not compel one to wholeheartedly regress towards infantile portions of personhood.

Another approach is to allow the context of their child to be domineering over their former families. As relic aspects of their former family emerge, the child may not respond in kind, indeed not being relevant or necessary according to the new environment. While other aspects can ascend for which parents have not allocated, that is from fissures of their own rearing, whereas the child may actively denounce them in spite of prevalence. These are aspects that the child cannot foresee, through intelligent inquiry would deduce them as aspects which are deserving attention. However, such erudition must be attended with the current situation in foresight; additionally with the intention of wholesome continued growth. The conflict between child and the parent's former family can be measured and identified when the child is forgotten from the equation or does not recognize adequate material to contest the environmental propositions. When the child is lost from the equation, being demoted from a childlike contender to a nonexistent entity then we can be sure that the proposition is a form of regression; all of its growth will undo far greater development which follows the succession of maturity.

Identity

Identity, when occupied too earnestly, can cause disruption of its intrinsic culture. Identity is a mere manifestation of all human culture, so when identity does not interact with that broader culture it loses its cultural value. Culture is the vessel containing human experiences, knowledge, beliefs, customs, and expressions. Since experiences, knowledge, beliefs, customs, and expressions are universal, a specific identity is a mere sample of that database. Any identity is informed by these universal features and when the relationship between identity and universality is fragmented, it can no longer be informed. The ensuing identity which thrives is able to be informed by the pre-existing culture, more significantly, to remain informed by a comprehensive access to the universal realm.

This can be noted by the intricate process which is necessary for a developing culture in making headway from the pre-existing one. The philosophical and theological dialogue which should habituate between them is paramount for both. This is an arduous process, which is specifically accounting for a continuation of the pre-existing culture's dialogue towards a more profound measure and to contrast a new identity. An identity does not arise from nonentities, and we can always record a dominant and primal identity which was formerly adopted which could cause the new identity to diminish. The former identity would find its way into the current conversation while delineating the novel and exposed identity by its side. Remembering that identity is the container of human experience and knowledge: better experience and knowledge would override substandard experience and knowledge. Therefore, an intellectual dialogue with the pre-existing culture was a process of embodying the pre-existing cultural identity into a new sphere of existence.

For the developing culture it would be sensible to corroborate with a pre-existing culture's ritual by mere fact that it was sourced in the pre-existing culture. Moreover, with a realistic transition in place, the lack of its incorporation can impair the developing culture.

Furthermore, we comprise little information about the depth or significance of a cultural aspect, and it may be that this rite holds considerable levity as a ritual that can transform the intellectual development of the developing culture. The developing culture may assert to not maintain conversation about the ritual by virtue of its pre-existing culture association, as if to simply imply that binding to archaic methods is an antithesis to progression. Rituals and intellectual material should be explored at face value without having a particular identity restricting the conversation and secondly, every cultural construct is built on preliminary models. Identity does not serve to limit interaction with the broader society, but rather as a placeholder to reside amongst the differing conversation.

The developing culture is to convey the pre-existing culture forward, albeit with some key tweaks and developments. Paradoxically, the ritual taken from the pre-existing culture can be part of a process which distinguishes them from the pre-existing culture. The new culture will enact subtle differences between cultures, for when performing the ritual in a different context it assumes a new origin. Similarly, the primary element of the pre-existing culture should be the quintessential aspect of the developing culture. By taking the highest point and applying it as a method for a new culture, it ensures the survival of both cultures.

A deficient pre-existing culture will usually profess familial symptoms, especially in reference to the suitable potential of the family structure. When certain characters of the familial body are apt to manifest their role, they are either suppressed or neglected. The deficient familybody would take a notion of significance contrary to that potential and apply their resources in a new direction despite the surrounding resentment.

The manner in which the parents interact with the aspect of significance deriving from the potential is to determine the status of an efficient familybody. This is coincided by the way the siblings take advantage of that sentiment which will define the constitution of the family. This constitution is made by those three authors, the superior parent and inferior parent as well as applied aspects that are tailored around the inadequacy of each sibling and parent in their relation to the center gravity of the family. The superior parent who did not meet the highest regard of the familybody will be engraved in the memory of the other members.

When the children do not meet the expectation of the superior parent, it will be engraved into the center gravity of the familybody. This will elucidate which pathway is necessary, with each member either taking the role of that missed expectation or embodying the existential essentials that weren't intersected. We understand this in terms of a deficient familybody by having the simplistic expectation become the overall experience of the setting. With either a portion of the family to perform it, or to be troubled by it, even as there is a vast amount of information that could be accessed despite that notion of the pre-existing culture.

For instance, ancient Greece would have the familybody fixated on citizenship facets. This would be a deficient familybody by neglecting the personal side of the equation, to the point of filicide and pedophilia which would be a point of conjecture had anyone perceived beyond political references.

A large familybody will naturally split into teams, with one side taking the role of expectation while the other of unmet needs. Each side will be requisite to enact that relationship, so that the side of expectation will attempt to foster despite the overarching expectation and the side of necessities will accept its existential deficiency. Eventually, the roles will shift, so that the conversation continues in a more profound manner.

A pre-existing culture in a state of deterioration would not be able or willing to make that shift and thus would be destined to stagnation and accentuating resentment. When families are of royal stature and there is much to gain and lose from where they are situated, the dynamic of these two roles will always manifest themselves in public conversation and individual intuition. This will lead either to the estrangement of the expectation or the estrangement of the superior parent. Societies which are attempting to point away from the degeneration would be advised to remove the expectation and evolve the culture.

This can be found in the dialogue between the developing culture and the pre-existing culture, as the pre-existing culture does not concern itself with rearing children and finds no need to have them partake in cultural service. The developing culture must have the children participate, the rearing of children fashions a community competent and progressive. The pre-existing culture itself is being ousted by their own cultural axioms, which has delinquents taking official roles: mirroring the neglect of the necessities that are continuously frustrated to be both rearing discontent and having the innate system vulnerable by being replaced by those who have not progressed.

The context of the pre-existing cultures primary axioms should be extensively elaborated throughout the program of the developing culture and should take part in all their lifestyle. Almost as if to take the same sincerity of the pre-existing culture with an additional level of depth. We must not take it lightly that a central foundation of the new culture is in relation to the failed ideas of the preceding cultures' doctrine.

The focus of attention within the existing culture shall be the interlocking moment that the culture shifts from one to another. For the United States, the communal memory of the 'Mayflower' and its travelers would be the instant of that transfer between cultures. That moment when the decadent pre-existing culture fades and the developing culture commences is essential for its longevity, e.g., retaining the city names of the pre-existing culture with the humble preface of 'new'. For the moment that the new doctrine ceases to connect to the interplay between cultures, the new culture loses its foundation.

To be accurately coupled to the pre-existing culture would hinder the creation of a new form. The adjustment from a prior to a new form occurs with a fissure, and the area between them is the most threatening aspect of the new culture. To transition from the timeworn tradition even with all the philosophical inquiry would still require a piercing separation that is irrational and unexplainable. There is an element of unknown when one goes through a state of metamorphosis, and there is a state between two states which retains a conceptual gap.

When the semen has been released but did not reach its terminus, it is an occurrence which is neither the progenitor nor the initial stages of new life. This mid-arena would still be considered regenerative life. At this moment, semen does not contain a new life form, as it is not attached to the progenitor, nor does it reside in a condition that will actualize its potential. The potential within semen is not considered life, or then we must consider all semen within an individual to be animation. We must also consider all potential ideas that ruminate throughout society even as they are not to be expressed or actualized.

There must be a space between the sperm and the ovum for the continuation of life to take place. This cannot be understood by rationality, as we have explained there is no inherent life force within semen. The progenitor assists in the direction and the nature of gravity facilitates its movements, still from the semen's perspective it must endure a gap. If the semen were to contain an articulation, it would recognize itself as going through a period that could not be rationally understood by itself.

We take it for granted that as an unbiased observer we could postulate that semen contains potential, yet this cannot be biasedly experienced. When one enters the arena between two definite entities or aspects, they will not be able sort rational sense. Therefore, a child, as an adult, will not be able to build a philosophical conjecture to fill the space between themselves and the progenitor. *Every human will always sense the existential fissure between themselves and their progenitor.* One can further their development by attempting to bond the fissure through philosophical and spiritual exercise, yet the space will always be there. One cannot afford a coherent proposition that will tranquil the entirety of selfhood.

A progenitor, on the other hand, could observe the offspring without this existential fissure. Being unbiased to a dependable degree allows to superintend the exact situation. They can make use of an understanding of potentiality and find solace in such explanations. This is one of the roles of the progenitor: to shape a complete theory that would account for the obvious breach between them and their offspring. This information will be intuitively imparted to the child and will assist in marking the fissure to be as minor as possible. We must understand that to form any line of reasoning as a third-party witness will always be inattentive from absolute rationality that would accompany one's possessive experience.

The fact that one is undergoing the state of experience has the mind working itself from within; and accordingly, there is no external marker from the beginning question to the final closure. When one is a witness or is perceiving from an external perspective, the commencing inquiries are external conditions that are brought inwardly, which thus has the mind toil the details. The external foundation does not allow the full scope of the mind's power since it eventually reaches an area that it does not intuitively understand.

For instance, one can find a rational approach to the transition from semen to higher life form, through theories such as potentiality and actuality. Yet, when the mind seeks to understand the 'state of experience' in respect to this potential, it draws a blank statement. Thereby, when the mind completes the formulation of the theory it does not include an individual experience of potentiality. The mind can search all phenomena for a contrast to potentiality but cannot experience such a state. When one "feels the potential" of something, they are categorically feeling the future vision that can blossom from the present moment. The state that is between them is not experienced and ascribing a feeling is not accurate.

This leads to the detail as such, in all experiences of metamorphoses requisites a sudden surge from one state to the other. This can be interpreted as entering the unknown, which is ascribing the neighboring feeling to that incoherent state; reaching out to the abyss without any assurance of landing anywhere. One can seek out a transcended narrative to fathom the process; to heighten their morale of this suddenness. Even so, the incorporation of the higher narrative does not remove the existential fissure and only appears as such.

When the state between two states is experienced, no selfhood exists within that realm. In some instances, one would be using the narrative to negate the reality of it until they have reached the actual abyss. Thereby, all the metaphysical incorporations also cease to exist. Once entering the state between states, one's mind ceases to be active and all conceptualizations cease to exist. Ultimately, one must face the abyss alone; devoid of selfhood, other beings, and narratives.

This points us to the primacy of the study of philosophy which is in service of comprehending as much of that experience as possible. With such an understanding, one will navigate such waters with deliberate and perfected choices. *Courage is the fortitude to leap, while philosophy is the knowledge to do it right.* As we have stated, if the developing culture deprived of deliberation had surged from the pre-existing culture they would have had their innate culture fragment. While, if they had forestalled it, they wouldn't have had a defined and distinct new culture.

Philosophy is the tool which would communicate when and how to perform such plunges into the abyss. The developing culture which endures dialogue with the pre-existing culture is celebrating the philosophical distinction between the dividing cultures. The depth and breadth of the philosophical understanding is what will remain impactful on the other side of the abyss. Everything that is not connected to the existential layers of an individual may be absent in the experience of metamorphosis. Philosophy covers all the existential layers and when tradition and culture are used in such a manner they are considered philosophy as well.

When the developing culture segregates without conveying the foundational elements from the pre-existing culture the results may be a strand of fragmented potential bits without synchrony. We can foreshadow that there will be endeavors to reincorporate with the pre-existing culture, a result due to an indifference to the relevance of the pre-existing culture. This is only natural, wanting to register for the fragments of their newfangled existence, having separated without closure. Alternatively, when they transition in a time-extensive manner, they are always avid to reform and revolutionize.

When the developing culture has made an existential error in the formation of their substructure, it would be incumbent upon them to have a ritual or custom to serve as a reminder of their vulnerability for the objective to invariably pursue that closure. The developing culture is built from this transitional moment, an attribute that will be effective as long as it remains in the program. The fissure between the two cultures failed to sufficiently integrate the foundational element of the pre-existing culture. Consequently, the implementation to exclude the pre-existing culture is also necessary, as the inherent base of the culture may seek absolute regression at a feeble moment. When the separation occurs with some equilibrium, the notion of reverting to the pre-existing culture is not intimidating, in consequence of being a mere modification to a predecessor.

The Islamic tradition can exemplify a culture that departed from its predecessor in a gradual procession. The measured transition prompted multiple Caliphates to restructure the tradition, driven by the Islamic sentiment that it must always be adapted, improved, and changed. The manner in which it began had generated the defining character of 'revolution' in its ensuing stages. The leader and the populace had taken an approach with hesitation to proceed in a direct and distinct manner from their former culture. This was the element that was absent from the existential leap. This notion exists throughout the tradition and served as a significant benefit on certain occasions.

The cultural haven that the Abbasid Caliphate resided was due to the inclination to make themselves accessible to participate and contribute to an expansive array of cultures and knowledge. Differing from Christian counterparts who were conscious of putrefying their identity. The Christian foundation was a comprehensive parting, having the withdrawal from the former culture as an immediate and rapid action. In the regular span of a transition to include a measured dialogue between the developing culture and the pre-existing culture, presiding over multiple generations of development.

That rapidity of Christian inception has necessitated an ongoing quest to compensate by pursuing to revert to its former culture. The extreme measure that medieval Christianity took against its members was to ensure their identity not disintegrate by regressing to the culture it had manifested from.

The Protestant Reformation was a setback to the traditionalist culture, a clear indication of returning to its former state. However, the identity did not disintegrate and rather served as an examination about the existential fissure between Christianity and its former culture. This was because it was completed through intellectual discourse and rationality, contrasted with a gothic negation of one's identity. Had they fully returned to the former culture it would have negated the culture, causing their status to be ensnared whereas the former culture was only accessed through the new culture. Having disintegrated the new culture, there wouldn't be a reason to maintain an allegiance to the former culture. They would have either despised the former culture for causing the disintegration or persisted with resentment towards their cultural foundations for not relating to its origins. Instead, they established a new locale to initiate a political system that resembles that modification.

The Islamic tradition can be categorized as the opposite of the Christian experience, by having the culture endure multiple states of metamorphosis. This would also be the cause of interruption, becoming vacant for too much change and losing its core identity. With this circumstance as a defying premise, a significant ritual for the Islamic tradition would be to recap the slow nature of the Islamic expansion. By remembering that attribute with the coinciding apprehension of an existential leap, they can remain conscious of the overcompensation brought about through excessively adapting.

Let us postulate two separate reasons for dealing with the existential fissure. The first, as mentioned, is the heightened morale and courage that is accessed in reaching out to a metaphysical narrative. Second, the metaphysical narrative as used to negate the reality of that existential fissure, and by doing so, to face as little of it as possible. This second motive is the fainthearted version of the first, for one is reluctant to deal with reality as it exists by using a narrative as a mode to negate it.

Similarly, a child shares all the same features of the parent yet still preserves a new form. The space which exists between child and parent is the most contentious and challenging component of the child's perceived existence. If the parent does not invest in the child's wellbeing as perceived by the child, then that space becomes emphasized, which entreats the question, from where does the child stem if the parents are not consciously attentive?

The child's individuation will be afflicted by either the failure of the parent to fulfill their needs or the demands which the parents have placed on the child. The expectation also emphasizes the fissure between them, as the parents are wavering their connection with expectations to fulfill. If the child chances those expectations, they experience less of that gap, alternatively, when unmet, the attachment to existence deteriorates.

Therefore, the space between the pre-existing culture and the newly formed developing culture is the most contentious and disruptive aspect of the developing culture. There is a constant need to find the interconnectedness between the two, whether by the pre-existing culture 'expectations' or 'needs' of the developing culture's populace under the pre-existing culture dominion. The developing culture begins the dialogue with the pre-existing culture to put to attention their needs, which were a part of the pre-existing culture's neglected population. The expectations of the pre-existing culture revolved around the pivotal parts of their thesis, which overlooked the other portions of their culture. Moreso, the expectations were to take account of certain dichotomies of perspective, with the developing culture including those and some more. They are to attend to the routine of the pre-existing culture, albeit with an inclusion of their particular needs.

The epochs of decadence for the developing culture can be viewed as either the fixation to enjoin the culture back to the pre-existing culture or an overindulgence in their requirements despite the pre-existing culture's expectation of them; even as they are bygone. This is quite an equilibrium, for if they followed the culture too strictly, they would revert to the pre-existing culture and if they had the current culture unkempt, they would fragment the novel developments. The solution to this predicament is to have the culture built upon that very area of contention. A definite portion of pre-existing culture should become the primary component of the developing culture.

Any culture is erected upon the familiarities of the moment that it transitioned from its former self so that the developing culture can never become misplaced between those two cultures. Thereby, any celebratory moment is always associated with that intermediary phase which stresses the attention towards the pre-existing culture and the modification from it. This is also the solution to the rift between progenitor and child, for when the familybody celebrates the birth, it highlights the existential transition between the two entities and the child will gain a semblance of existence. The mere prominence of the fissure testifies to the duality of its existence which emphasizes one to tend to both realms.

The occupation of the developing culture was not to delegitimize the pre-existing culture since that would only demonstrate intellectual and physical prowess. Having left all the pre-existing culture behind, the mere memory of banishing the pre-existing culture would not outweigh the extensive impact of the current model. Had the developing culture proceeded without being absorbent with a dialogue with the existing pre-existing culture, their new identity would have instantly become secluded from broader culture. The measured process attests to the requirement of not divorcing from one's identity, instead, in transforming it.

We may wonder why it was considered to the detriment of the developing culture with their regression to revert to the pre-existing culture. This can be viewed as a petition to return to the former culture, claiming that despite the modifications, it is a more dominant and elaborate culture. Four self-refuting arguments are at play. Firstly, if a culture absolutely retains dominance, its influence and power would be evident through its natural manifestation without the need for explicit assertion. By asserting dominance, especially in the form of an intellectual debate, one inadvertently raises doubt about its authentic dominance, since dominance should be apparent.

Secondly, when one asserts that a culture is more dominant, they are making a claim about its level of influence or superiority. However, if one desires to engage in a dialogue about a dominant culture, it immediately should be supported by evidence or demonstration of real control and influence. Without the intellectual basis, the argument becomes self-refuting, as if one must revert to an ethos to prove its sensibility. Dominance of culture, by nature, cannot be argued with ethos as culture is the container of human learning. When asserting dominance of social learning, higher social learning should be the topic of conversation not a nostalgic ethos.

Thirdly, when a culture is the dominant pendulum of the future, it is already at the pinnacle of influence within any given context. The influence is due to its superior expansion in terms of its breadth of consciousness, which has a more profound effect on the individuals who engage it. The manner in which the Romans, after conquering the Greeks, became subservient to the more prolific Hellenistic culture. Despite the physical supremacy they yielded to their adversaries, by virtue of the Greeks having the superior culture causing the entirety of Rome to essentially come to be them.

When one resides in a secondary culture and speaks in reference of the dominant culture, by stating their own dominance refutes itself. There aren't levels of dominance, since dominance implies a singular superior position. There is a fundamental binary nature to dominance: a culture is either dominant or it is not. Once outside the role of dominance, they remain in the background without any centric status. When one postulates that a pre-existing culture is more dominant, they are assenting to be equals, since two cultures contending for dominance cancel out a singular for being dominant.

Fourthly, when in conversation about a dominant culture, there is a power-dynamic which will ultimately assert one over the other. Until that moment arises, admitting that there is a power-dynamic becomes a clear demonstration that the role of dominance is not definite. The power balance becomes more of a competition rather than a clear hierarchy. Thus, in this preliminary stage, it should be the cause of introspection and not the call for actively asserting one culture over another. The demand to return to the pre-existing culture, an active decision, should have been a moment of introspection as to the cultural significance of each.

The Decadence of Dialogue

The peril of an identity is the utilization of its organization in deference to the rest of personhood. The potency of identity is that it can provide a relief locale to compact a realistic situation. Thus, identity can be used to mitigate all the conflicting and contentious aspects of a non-identity experience. Contradicting this notion, identity may also fail to provide any deliverance that would be worthy of its expenditure. Identity is much like a cave, to retreat when externalities become existentially demanding, during which there is no alternative dialogue, for it is only in service of its safety provision that would not jeopardize any aspect with a positive amount of enlightenment.

To be more exact of this proposition we will explore a theoretical dialogue and pinpoint the items of interest for this discussion. The commencement of the conversation might launch their position within the context of an identity. This initiation is despite the relevancy of the discussion to be always a manifestation of the universal experience of personhood, beyond the fringes of an identity. As the dialogue progresses, an attempt is made by either proponent to elaborate into a sphere that is existentially relevant, demanding a certain root aspect of the psyche to self-reflect and deliberate.

During such dialogue, most proponents will be attentive to the needs and objectives of the conversation as to avoid encroaching on non-dogmatic aspects of selfhood and thus contention and conflict will not ascend. The constitution of the identity and every subsequent conversation concerning its elements is to ensure that the existential self is sheltered. It would be a troublesome experience to have the content of the identity serve against its purpose and mount unnecessary existential developments.

However, when either proponents are reluctant to abide by this code of conduct, one will begin to press into the context to compel a general formation of an existential touch which will arouse an existential movement and revolutionize both individuals. When a side of the discussion reaches a precipice which initiates the flowering of an outer existential layer, the continued response will inaugurate a new dialogue, one existentially tolerable.

In a certain sense, this begins when the content of the conversation is made aware as a universal aspect of experience and is not confined to the identity's parameters. Additionally, enduring an existential demand creates the realization that identity cannot be in service to the continuation of the dialogue. This will entreaty the respondent to shift apparatuses to the universal nature of their existence; to approach an existential aspect of personhood in relation to that.

Averse to abide by such a demand, the respondent will attempt a dogmatization of the dialogue to which the identity has not conjured thus far. The sentence which brought the shift in dialogue cannot be found within the library of the identity, as is the case of all existential dealings, being profound aspects of personhood; novel and unknown. To avoid the proper continuation of the dialogue, the respondent will extract a dogmatic idea from the identity that is wholly fused with an aspect of that newly exposed existential layer.

When the next sentence is formulated, it will usually be inconsistent with the previous point due to the mental entanglements of extracting content from the identity to be included with the present exposure of existential revelation. It may be so illogical from the sequence of conversation that it would be impossible to respond in a coherent fashion and thus the dialogue discontinues. To continue, one must be aware of both the respondents' existential layers and the process by which they went and sought content from their identity. This was all performed by the respondent to propose that the conversation has not shifted its theme; the identity is apparently universal, lacking no existential dread.

Even as the respondent experiences an existential layer, they will assume the burden and project it into the library of the identity and produce a supposedly perfected response to which the identity had no difficulty to deal with. This is an enacted version of forfeiting the existential layer of themselves in order to protect the identity, which ironically is only important to the respondent because the identity promises existential safety. The logicality is that the existential sacrifice of this thin layer is worthwhile to avoid an even more in-depth development of existential dread.

Another approach for a respondent is to accept the context of the conversation, although to be under the rubric of identity, verifiably to be also a universal conversation. Therefore, it doesn't require to be anchored to the identity and could thus remain free to explore the unknown factor through the lens of universal experience. Yet, there is still the existential wound which has taken effect and cannot be solved with exploration of non-identity attachments. Parallel to a non-identity conversation which can also expose existential depth, entreating the proponents to engage in something novel and contentious for the residing culture. Even in the universal realm, although less constricting than the identity, there remains a style of identity that endorses certain tenets and facets.

For instance, as freedom is a contemporary tenet, infiltrating the philosophical basis behind freedom and the nature of the relationships between individuals will enter existential territory that will entice an aspect of concrete personhood to demand fundamental change and deliberation. Because such a concept is highly consecrated for contemporary universality, the existential depth that may be exposed would be attractive despite its uncharted waters.

However, if we were to explore a less profound and newly formulated concept such as equality, even as the existential exposition has a similar shape, it will not be charmed for further dialogue because there is apprehension one will be unable to return to the center of the idea and may even find a wasteland of philosophical backing. Therefore, the universal apprehension towards existential exploration is not about cowardice as would an identity, but in order to ensure that the tenets are protected to a certain degree as to avoid an unsettling political structure with too much variation or philosophical fractures.

The respondent can approach the dialogue from a non-identity standpoint but will only be available to the discussion as prepared for two factors; one the personal inclination to enter and formulate within structural selfhood, and two, the manner to perceive universal experience in terms of their encircled construct. Each individual has a different esteem towards universal experience which may contain presumptions that are concealed as an identity.

For instance, certain social norms and cues may be so paramount for some that an observer would presume they were following a traditional solidification of rules and prohibitions. During a universal engagement, such individuals will be reluctant to be fluid in a wholesome interaction. This is not because they worry about the existential dread as would be characteristic of an identity but precisely because of their presumption that universal parameters are part of the universal system.

The nature of universality is starved of parameters, yet to adhere to them as if they existed in parallel sequence contradicts itself. When we point this out, they may shift into existential territory and begin a formation of nihilistic rhetoric. For them, the existential territory is a haven to not disrupt their version of reality. They may take a satirical or comical methodology payable to the masking of their existentiality with a certain mocking of general existence. The point of the matter is the same, for they are very hesitant to restructure reality.

The notion of questing reality is assumed to be upsetting, not for the existential layers that may be exposed but because an altered reality must be equivocated with a change in choices. The dread is one of a changed activity, which is not a fear of unknown sentiment as much as the transformation of self-perception. An individual who performs major changes in their activity will inevitably perceive personhood in a different fashion.

This change will compel one to experience themselves as would a third-party observer, losing their first-perspective stance. This is dreaded for the replacement of selfhood with other forms of selfhood that will not shield respective developments within the current social system. This is a fairly rational fear to which the protective edge is a surrounding social environment that will receive the new persona with a certain animosity and thus become dynamically opposed to forward progress. Instead, they will be activating the voice of their prior self so that there is the possibility of incorporating many of the most cherished former components into their new existence.

When this is done with efficiency, which is to follow the existential process in light of the social disappointment, one will no longer necessitate such a social environment and will be adjusted by their intuitive recognition that they are representing unnecessary elements and thus adapt to a more progressive entourage. Another approach to effectuate this process is for one to readjust the entire social sphere to meet standards that would dynamically oppose for a more wholesome personhood to perpetuate adequate progressive growth.

Therefore, the fear of a newfound self-perception is in tandem with a problematic social environment which would duly protect prior selfhood. This problematic environment can be caused either by a hesitancy of the constituents to represent their connections for productivity of the social circle, or more commonly, a lack of diversity or availability in the social surroundings to be a shelter for such transitions. Diversity is necessary due to the fact that a single-minded group would be considered a single individual for an existential occasion, despite the supremacy of the multitudes.

Another development for a problematic social environment is the lack of affair for the welfare of social connections, thus, to provide existential shelter is not something to be risked. Theoretically, a dialogue would endure indefinitely in an enlightening fashion if both proponents were existentially prepared and retain the availability for restructuring reality with a continuous modification of self-perception. This would be successful only if the social sphere meets certain aforementioned standards.

Proposal for Identity

Between the biological identity that makes up the familial affiliate and the universal exposure of the persuading culture, we encounter a breach of sorts. The differentiation arises due to the exact need of a universal formation for biological identity. To comprise a capacity to interact with universality with only a modest biological identity, one constructed by the familial body, would not suffice because of a deficient intellectual complexity. While to make a bid at universality from an identity stance with a combination of the two; for instance, a political movement, would be the grounds for a departure from the biological class which is vital of an austere identity.

The primary notation of this criterion is that it must be biologically linked. When this characteristic is missing, it would degenerate the familial attachments with a headlong approach toward universality. Absolute universality is relentlessly stirring and cannot be pinned into a formation which would make it worthwhile of an interaction. The most we can do is set up a domain that can receive such exposure without demeaning its potency or vitality. A structure that is exacted with many subtle impediments would simply contract the reception of that flow. The attempt at furthering the domain by declaring a point of interaction and adding a formulation of vitality of its own, makes the entire domain lose its overall receptivity. What remains is an aide-mémoire of that universality that is not critical, exhibited for all to perceive. Biological receptivity can diminish exponentially to be incapable of retaining any intimacy.

Whichever domain facilitates to obtain whichever universality becomes a habitat of biological necessities that materializes to obtain that universality by its complex structure for receptivity and proximity. The degree of that biological interaction is the vacancy and sentimental receptivity to be exposed from that universality. There is a limited range of biological elements such as sustenance, rest, housing, sociality, lighting, and sexual intimacy.

Identity does not effort to be a receptive agent for that universality, for it is not a physical structure. Identity proposes itself as a biological agent which can interact with universality for the expanded subjectivity of the individual. Instead of being a conceptual domain to receive universality, it stands by itself as a biological component so that in all our biological interactions we would incorporate that conceptual layer. This process has the great ability of receiving every bit of that expanded conceptual layer, that which is partial to the biological system. This is done by creating the illusion that it is biologically justified.

The only setback to such a feat is that we must convince the constituents of the identity that these conceptual layers are the entirety of their existence. This would generate the conceptual layer to be incorporated as part of their biological system. The biological system appears quite vibrant in its parameters. To incorporate such an expansive conceptual layer, the identity must appear as the only manner to interact with biological selfhood and the only expression of existence. The intimacy that is realized within an identity's biological scheme is received from absolute universality because one interacts with universality without choice. The conceptual layers of the identity are naturally rearranged to receive that universality to accord real intimacy.

The requirement of the identity is to reframe the perceptual-existence to be shaped into its parameters; analogous to when children perceive their progenitors as their entire existence. Therefore, identity is correspondingly relevant for children for they perceive their familial structure as an expansive unit of their biological self; another mode to describe identity. As the child enters maturity they will begin to experience absolute universality, to which the identity proves to be a limitation in their exploration. Even so, the mature adult will necessitate perceiving their biological state in a conceptual manner so that all information within their experience will be received with truthful intimacy.

However, this process can disrupt the reality framework that has been exposed during the coming-of-age. Identity can be used as a contextual library to perceive ahead towards universality. When used for the experience of intimacy, one which relies on the assumption of it being a singular existence, it becomes a deviation from wholesome personhood.

Within an identity, the intimacy arrives through contextual layers from universality. The contextual layers differ from other forms of context as they presume personhood to provide its existential provision for an auto symbiotic interaction. Thus, personhood will be defined by those intimate experiences and the personal realm in not part of the equation. To include the personal realm, the identity must restructure as an existential-contextual layer which serves the purpose of interacting with universality.

When any context is appreciated from a non-localized place, we will naturally perceive it through any level of our biological formation and identity protects us from this. For instance, if one perceives a certain traditional understanding of the concept of work, they can restructure that context which deviates from the truth of personhood. However, the notion of work is a universal theme, so that a context regarding its structure which arrived from an infantile locale is now appropriated to another context. The depth of this context is not because of the existential link but due to an elaborate study that culminated in the universal realm. We acknowledge that the study is vitalized from a certain immaturity, however, the final context is perceived as part of the adulted version.

The biological layer is complemented by connecting the identity to the familial structure, to which it espouses this peculiar conceptual domain with the coinciding property of both biological and conceptual. The family unit is an abstract construct that participates in regular universality, nevertheless, stays attentive and communicates the details of immediate biological necessities. The identity incorporates itself into the family structure to define its members alongside a conceptual expanse. The family itself cannot perform an apparatus such as this for they don't retain the biological resources to granulate all that conceptual information. The identity expands the human footprint with the assumption of a biological bond, thereafter can search for a conceptual expanse, one which does not become misplaced in a community dynamic.

Identity is a receptive domain, not unlike the matter of constructing a domain. This understanding will correlate to what is characteristic of an identity. To sustain considerable realization for a receptive domain it must comprise a higher-life-form representation for biological alignment. The representation must be assured in perfect order without an overtly personal realm to spout a single being and their persona. The first chamber must be large and available to multiple areas so that it doesn't compel short interaction nor a stationary state that would cause too much personal relation through recognition and interaction. An identity is of the same fabric, as the more private, personal, or particular it becomes, the more diluted is its receptivity. (In a forthcoming work 'Representations')

The second component is biological intimacy which if not considered would prove the structure of no value. Therefore, one may enter for a state of respite, so that when respite occurs it is done for its biological necessity. Sexual intimacy is more effective of a biological interaction to contrast sleep which entails less mental interaction. We may assume that sexual intimacy to be the cause of a volatile personal practice that will remove the individual from universal receptivity. This is the circumstance when intimacy lands from a relational aspect between proponents. However, when sexuality is biologically aroused and contextually stimulated, it has the criteria of an 'animal', causing the enmeshment of biological and contextual layers. They would parallel themselves to the structure or context. Identity does the work of integrating the sexual domain to inhabit a certain identity presence, effective according to the aforementioned. (In a forthcoming work, 'Critical Sexual Theory', 'Context and Intimacy')

Third component - A contextual layer for sexual interaction is the doorway contained by the chamber to receive what is in the room. When sexual interaction is stimulated through relationship material, as a form of love for instance, it will be relatable in its particular depth, yet would be removed from the surrounding environment because of a personal bias. Even as the biological manifestation seems to be a subjective expression it is still the nature of universality. There is nothing peculiar to a particular individual for their animalistic expression nor is it unique. The contextual layer is necessary for the receptivity of that structure, while the biological layer is merged for the climax of ultimate reception.

Forth - The domain is required to be placed in a universal location which is detailed to the uppermost arena of universal expression. Too near to that universality would regurgitate itself as an intrinsic part of that universality deprived of receptivity, one that must shy away from it. Social representation is fairly important to allow the structure to appear as a biological interaction, so that the representation should incorporate a slight exhibition of a higher life form without denoting a personal basis. Identity's selection of physical location follows the same logicality. (In a forthcoming work, 'Center of Universality', 'Elements of Civilization')

Identity enlarges the biological layer to include the conceptual jurisdiction, while absolute universality and its receptive domain will utilize its context to interact with universality. They would be formatted with a biological layer to secure its integration. The contextual layer is the only manner to appropriately interact with universality, to which we will always agree that a child's education must be highly contextualized.

Without such adhering context, the child will interact with the universal realm with the remaining context from infantile suppositions. If there is a certain discontent with femininity at an infantile stage, the child will interact with the universal realm according to that fixation. We could still presume the interaction to be an absolute piece of universality, but we could just as well say this about any interaction. The resolution of the interaction is to receive as much content from universality as personhood has the capacity to retain. While a child will be positioned with a highly contextualized education in which their interaction with the universal realm is restricted, as maturity takes effect, one gains the capacity to interact with more of that universality. Therefore, the mature one will remove those burdening contextual layers and have them reconstructed to advance toward more content and less constraint. Comparable to this very discussion, which voices through a context that is versatile and can be adapted to more aspects of universality.

The next sentence will demonstrate the departure of coherent context. "In the prose of continual cyclical nature, the avoidance of reciprocity is highly ineffective as a result." The sentence can still be understood; however, its context is too broad for rigorous interaction. When we analyze and obtain an understanding, we will create an improved version of the content. This analysis will be different than the intended sentence and a personal context will make it coherent. For instance, we can understand this as: 'goodness has its limitations', even as this wasn't my intended sentiment.

We will propose a sentence that is perfect for the immature mind but is burdening to the mature one. 'Sit when eating'. Although this is a contextual layer to interact with food consumption, the understood context is that one shall sit during eating. It does provide a perceived idea of behavior regarding eating but limits food interaction to a specific position. However, we could expand the context so that it serves a broader context. We could expound that food consumption is an intense biological process which deserves a physical ritual that separates it from other daily activities. Although this is not necessarily the intended meaning, we can devise a personal take and improve it without limiting our horizon.

Identity and its Symmetry

Identity serves as a locale to insularly exist and is presumed to be the only reality, much like the homebody is assumed to be a solitary experience. The homebody assumes the temporal site to be central for its members, even if such is not the correct reality of the circumstance, as noted in political unrest. The homebody can provide for a sense of a reality for its various benefits, in addition, identity does so in the conceptual realm.

Identity surveys their arena in terms of the universal details of current consciousness. While being unable to label any of these details, for instance, the manner to interact in the public domain, it shadows the flow of conversation incapable to halt and reflect as if it were the only locale of interaction.

Without identity, the manner of interaction within the public domain will be based on the present details of the universal conversation. While universality will prepare an outline for interaction with the public, it entails without an embodied experience of those details inasmuch as it cannot embody anything. If we were to say, "respect," we do not achieve enough details for daily interactions which are far more complex than an axiom can conjure. Even if the universal conversation is specifically focused on those details, hence ready to unpack the axiom, it will never cover the nuances and personal aspects that are always relevant to a specific situation.

Identity allows for the mitigation of this problem, being another layer of perception that interacts with proposed universally. For instance, to be polite is an axiom, moreover, identity can interact with the axiom by being a codex of detail which distills the information. The identity provides an assumed reality structure that will be available to simmer the information in becoming personal and relatable. It does not follow the rules of austere reality which will pilot away from those details given that it is not the composite picture. Instead, it will underscore the concept of politeness with its entire enterprise of assumed realistic notions, for which one will visit and embody the interaction; teaching daily details of applied politeness in their behavior. They will understand a sense of self related to the axiom which parallels the sociality, allowing a more thorough and proper course of action.

There are pockets of consciousness that deserve attention that will not be manageable by the universal exploration of consciousness. They get mishandled because the universal realm abides by an outstanding exploration that cannot detail all that passes. To cover these realms requires a system that assumes reality for the present moment, provided that consciousness can only be had when it becomes the primary notion of reality. When it is merely an instance of intellectual stimulation, it does not allow the existential mode of selfhood to participate. Secondly, identity requires a form of civilization to distribute and embody the assumed reality, comparable to how absolute civilization is required for the progress of consciousness.

1-For illustration, the universal realm has uncovered a focal capacity of consciousness in the department of sexuality. Alternatively, it had unheeded the distribution process which in consequence had the realm of immodesty infiltrate its infantile inhabitants, owing to the reception of an impartial analysis of sexuality, despite shame being an organic instinct. The letdown of this elaboration can be had with various identities taking upon themselves as reality frameworks, gaining a communal backing to provide the civilized attribute albeit only for the distribution fissure of the underdeveloped population. The material misplaced from consciousness can then be reinserted into the consciousness system. Theoretically, one can follow the details of universal sexual development and identify that fracture. However, to detail and provide a conscious layer to that realm, one which had been realized and actualized on the periphery of the social system, would require an attachment to an identity for such a provision. More likely is the case, identity will be used to deviate from the universal realm by articulating that modesty is the sole method to perceive sexuality, consequently denouncing all the consciousness that has evolved in that realm.

2-Another case in point of this would be the conscious reception of a political establishment. Under the establishment, it would be impossible to outline the political structure in its realistic mainframe, being as one is an existent participant. Therefore, participation in another political identity is essential to interact with the embodiment of the new civilization which alternates to diplomatically interact with the outline of one's innate political entity. We acknowledge with scientific certainty that the foremost leaps of human evolution coincide with the great migrations from Africa.

3-A third illustration would be consciousness in reference to the ancient notion of sacrifice. Although contemporary civilization is participating, it does so from under a concealed locale which does not embrace the various details which produce accurate results. This could be the very reason that it has been avoided, being that it became so integrated within the system that denoting a particular nuance may be assumed to decline the embodied performance. However, with the absent details, there is a waiting wearying to occur.

An identity will be of service, especially the religious identities, to provide an entire conscious enterprise to surround this notion. When approached to be applied to the missing information in the universal realm, it becomes a validation of something that seems missing. Of course, we find such an exploration to be pursued further than this validation, instead of a filler to a more important conversation it converts to an insulated conversation which deviates from the course of universality. This would be a natural course of direction, as the only way we can validate the existential self is to assume the identity to be the entire assumed reality. Thus, to divorce from that would be to face one's existential bareness, for a moment at least, in order to transition from an assumed reality to an actual reality. This is compulsory for all higher life forms, however, to deliberately choose such a track is quite demanding.

4-We can find such a pattern with Freud who had charted the consciousness surrounding dreams, one which had been repressed due to its religious associations. Shaping those mental representations from religious realms to follow its inherent consciousness until it was able to be reunited with the universal conversation. Even as such, there remain certain breaches in the exploration due to the personal bias to navigate away from its religious associations. When a dream forecasts the future it is not only a wish-fulfillment, being that it subconsciously conducts the individual to follow a sequence of events which seek out that future. Almost as if the future is already in the individual's dominion, with only the regulator buried deep within the substructure. The dream is the manifestation of that mechanism of control which will enact the future, unbeknownst to the person. Although the environment seems external and cannot be organized by an individual, there will be a near-infinite amount of interactions that will affect the environment to produce those results. Thus, we can analytically determine the future of one's lifespan except when they follow those inborn fundamentals which manifest in those dreams. Conversely, this analysis may contain a certain deviation based on my avoidance owed to biases and resentments, which has another researcher track this to a more comprehensive state.

5-*An example of identity* being used to uncover an element which has not been adequately addressed in the universal system is the physical structure of a home. The finite details which encircle the structure that have not been afforded by the architectural field, covering the intuitive sense and not its complete intellectual elaboration. The intuitive sense would assert that the entrance should have high ceilings and open space. Intellectual elaboration would detail the beginning of a representation to be its availability, especially considering that the home is based on its interaction with the external realm that joints at this room. The availability of the home must interact with the strangeness of the external realm to allow that representation to take effect. This is beyond the field of architecture as the discipline halts its exploration in the final function of the structure. Therefore, we can identify a concept that encompasses that liminal area of research, perceiving the homebody as a dynamic system that both decays and prospers regardless of its location and structure. When the location changes, as does daily, the structure must adapt accordingly. This dynamic interplay between internal and external realms can be thoroughly examined through a specific identity.

6-*Moreover, identities often contain stipulations* that do not prioritize and display consciousness. For example, many major identities have specific viewpoints on alcohol. Despite their prescribed procedures for engaging with this substance, the conscious offering is reclusive to relevant material for the universal conversation. The stipulation might contain a degree of conscious understanding that has been overshadowed by the rule itself. The stipulation may in fact be followed with rigor because universal consciousness that is in reference to this substance surpassed the identity's meager exploration of it.

Instead, we should adhere to the higher consciousness and its ensuing fissures, allowing identities to cover the breaches. To extend the example, although universal consciousness towards alcohol is exemplary, it does not necessarily translate into effective rituals. An identity can provide a conscious layer that details the precise approach to alcohol in a communal setting.

The ability to discern what constitutes a gap within consciousness in comparison to actually being a foundational element comes through interaction with the universal realm. When consciousness has reached a position to embrace alcohol as not being an everyday beverage, we cannot assume this impression to be a breach to be otherwise relegated by an identity. This is something that can be detailed in its complexity by the universal conversation and does not have the characteristic of a decadent conversation. We could have an identity which contains a wide-ranging elaboration of alcohol but only in consequence of interacting with every detail of the universal perspective, and subsequently this trait would define it as a determinate perspective.

The only incentive for an identity to perform this act of defiance is through frustrating attempts at satisfying, dealing, or distressing with the fissures without reprieve. Without a hopeful response, the breaches become so significant for which the identity activates to take over an entire element of consciousness.

7-*We are going to enter* by way of example to understand a further point. Food customs are the cornerstone to most prevalent identities, including familybodies. This is because the universal conversation cannot cope with dietary necessities and its details. The universal realm is always evolving and food traditions are private and rely on varying familial elements that cannot be included in the public domain. However, this does not mean that the universal realm does not have a stake of consciousness in reference to food details. For instance, wild animals are generally not considered appropriate for consumption. This understanding stems from a certain degree of conscious awareness; if we were to delve to the credence, we might uncover a reasoning in respect to the wild nature being unsuitable for higher-life-form consumption, or the ambiguity and repulsion surrounding insects being of a criteria that is undefined, being neither exclusively associated with animal or plant.

However, most identities are far more elaborate in dietary consciousness and can be a source to fill these gaps. Despite the lack of expansion in the universal realm, it will always remain the elemental base for dietary understanding. Only after the universal perspective has been effusively explored can we seek the gaps for which an identity can address.

An example is contemporary consciousness surrounding animal consumption. Even though identities have long postulated a whole edifice on animal sacrifice and the culinary practices involving meat in certain commemorative events, the elemental base must still be the universal consciousness. While one can survey the complete disallowance for an animal product and identify a conscious cavity of the details and relevancy of certain animal consumption, the citation is only deserving when it had tolerated the comprehensiveness of the universal voice.

8-*We may ask if there is any other necessity* for identity other than covering the cavities of consciousness. While the sole purpose, identity has the other benefit of allowing universal reality to be experienced via an assumed reality. This becomes quite questionable in the meantime as we are using an assumed reality to platform an experienced reality and subsequently dismissing the very reality it attempts to emulate. For example, the traditional experience that is garnished by an identity produces a sense of nostalgia from a former period and its universal consciousness. For the reason that not all consciousness is transferred from one generation to the next, the embodiment of an earlier period will contain strands of consciousness which can be considered breaches for the universal realm of contemporary society.

For instance, a traditional cuisine perhaps with attention on a vegetable or seasoning. That former generation may have endured a climate or environment that would benefit from an influx of a certain aspect. Furthermore, this aspect represents the entire culture and its developed consciousness. That culture surely contains morsels of consciousness to furnish the missing aperture of present universality. However, to follow that traditional experience may exclusively adhere to gaps of present universality, beginning to denounce the foundational base of contemporary culture. A dosage of that culinary experience would be enough for the process to not betray foundational universality, all in accordance with the level of individual maturity.

When an emphasis on bread is misplaced, any identity can monitor this conceptual conflict. However, when the universal realm has covered a certain department, for instance, meat preparation, then every identity must forget its traditional method unless it can prove to provide a missing element. When starch and meat are positioned in a sandwich within contemporary culture, then every subculture which retains an equivalent should be discounted unless it can make the claim of a missing component. We understand the most important food choice of the universal realm by natural craving, and we can postulate a philosophy pertaining to its relevance. (Elaborated in another work, 'Food Consciousness')

The Transition

The drudged individual must reach beyond the natural conception and find a plateau of respite which is incoherent of selfhood. In the ideal scenario, they reason that by embracing their freedom even as only a posture of confidence, it will provide a familiarity of an enhanced self. They hope to be able to revisit and cover the intermediary space between the drudged psyche and a sophisticated perception. An enslaved individual, while remaining in the environment of servitude, cannot engage in abstraction and reach beyond servitude towards a conceptual coexistence. This is because bondage does not retain the capability to reach into the abstract intellectual sphere without a change of their intrinsic enslaved identity. More importantly, the relinquishment of the identity would be the cause of existential disarray, which they aren't formalized to handle; coupled with the fact that they lack other modes of existential safety to retreat upon.

The scenario becomes paradoxical, for a drudged one cannot maintain the fortitude to strive for freedom whilst cumbersome with dark matter and its requisite to approach its domain via intellectual growth. This is where a narrative measures in, with the bondaged individual turning outside themselves to the abyss of existential array, finding an active narrative to latch onto. That is, until they can find comfort in this new identity and become available to return to the history of their development. With the confidence as a free person and the fortitude to resurface the bygone, they can mend the two identities with rationality and philosophy. Likewise to any advancement that requires training; to be defined for this context as 'a responsibility for a new identity'. Once an individual is sufficiently trained, they can then classify the disparity between selfhoods, one prior to this identity and the version that has been imposed.

Military training exemplifies this well, as its primary objective is not to generate combatants but individuals who identify as combatants. The recruit who does not weave with that identity will be considered ineffective, while the one who may be lethargic in the corporeal aspects will be negotiable. Once the combatant comprises the identity which can be called to activation without hesitation, then the combatant can become an absolute combatant.

This entails the mending of the self which formerly did not partake in this identity, coinciding with the one that has been incorporated in present time. Many philosophical inquiries can be regaled as to the nature of war, courage, and nationality. With due time, the combatant would be engaging in warfare, not solely based on the identity of training but because this identity has communicated the philosophical nature of a combatant to other aspects of personhood. The reason that it must be philosophical is that the higher life form resides in the existential dark matter which has one constantly concerned with the fundamental nature of things. Something extraordinary must take precedence for the transition to be effective and vigorous, so as to not degrade into a facade of a presumed conscripter who performs like an enslaved person, especially when faced with the intensity of situations.

A drudged proponent becoming the presumed agency without transformation is politically upsetting. Enslaved individuals view their existence as a subsidiary of another being or beings, which makes them deeply dependent in regards to the existential layer of being. They rely on the conductor to navigate the harsher waters of life, the inquiries of meaning, direction, and purpose. In the tradeoff, the enslaved one tends to a narrow framework of experience, as if the entirety of the enslaved personhood was the hand of the handler. While the handler tends to all the complex components of their body and psyche, the enslaved tasks with the handler's hand alone and never deviates from it.

When an enslaved one reaches beyond their narrow framework, it would be comparable to a child facing adulthood in a single moment. The amount of learning and experience is immense and requires a time-lapse and commitment. The truth is that the enslaved, like any other beings, face existential disarray. However, the role of servitude limits their ability to have the dialogue to manifest such dealings. The presumed agency finds that the waning of the drudged one's role would allow for existential sincerity to manifest and that would be too dynamic for them.

The presumed agency may worry about the enslaved populace in their gain to power for multiple reasons, firstly, they will lose the hand of the enslaved and the associated material which it produces. Secondly, the position of the presuming agency may begin to be examined, which up to this point was secure. When an enslaved becomes free, the conscripter must air the existential question of their distinct role in society. The enslaved was offering the handler a sense of identity, which assisted against the existential dark matter they previously endured.

When the role of an enslaved individual becomes questioned, it proposes the conscripter into a similar struggle with their private identity. It is no wonder that the usage of scripture would be the most effective argument for slave owners of the American South; in having to face the existential disarray that would have been undecorated through freeing the enslaved.

Historian Larry Hise notes that ministers wrote almost half of all defenses of slavery. They listed hundreds of men of the cloth who used the Bible to substantiate that certain people were entitled to enslave individuals. Much approximating the pre-existing culture who can be understood as avoiding an advanced degree of existential disorder to be innocent in what was familiar. [i]

Moreso, and one which the pre-existing culture seems to maintain a stance, the enslaved will overtake the handler, existentially more than literally. The conscripter tends to the philosophical underpinnings of life, handling the oversight of human flourishing. Aristotle points out the role of a handler as managing the abilities of the subordinates. Stating that since such a task is "not great or wonderful," "for the handler need only know how to order that which the enslaved must know how to execute." "While the handler should dedicate their leisure beyond the home, with the pursuits of higher intellectual learning, namely philosophy and matters of the state." [ii]

This, I believe, was ill-considered, as the handler, in order to manage the subordinates, must tend to the intellectual component contributing to the interior of the home. The subordinates are the branches of the handler, so that the 'mind' of the homebody is left to deteriorate. If the handler would desert the confines of their home, the enslaved would be performing without an adequate leader.

Aristotle might conjecture that the conscripter returns home to bring along the educated experience which was established. Therefore, with the existential disorder that the house must deal, the needs are handled. The intricacy is why the conscripter must initially leave the homebody, being that the home requisites an available mind which can extend true mastering. Earlier in that work stating that the state is the replica of the homebody so that all the necessary astuteness for the state is a theoretical derivate of the homebody.[iii]

We conclude that the adage does not hope for the homebody to become an animated transcendent being. The outside realm is the only purposeful world. As a collective society, we have transitioned away from this ancient perspective and became cognizant of the sanctity of the individual and their home dwelling.

To illustrate this, the enslaved within the household are tasked to prepare the nutrition that will be served to the household members. This task is accomplished through the discipline of culinary arts with various gradations of expertise. The handler's body becomes dependent on the nutriment that is being served, in that it provides proper sustenance. The handler is also dependent on the subtle effects of a perfected dish based on the environment of the handler. If the conscripter has traveled a long distance, a certain dish will assist in calming the senses endured from the journey, while another dish will exasperate the body. The winter will necessitate more seasonings to heat the body, while the summer will do with less. A protein-dense diet will cause the conscripter to be intellectually sluggish while a starch-dense diet will cause the conscripter to be hypersensitive. The emotional energy of the day might call for a certain dish which can either serve to alleviate the stress or overburden it. A major occasion with an improper meal plan could stifle the conversation stream and its developments. In fact, we could create a whole science of the subject, which surely an enslaved person is not intellectually astute to formulate. Since the conscripter is not shadowing intellectual extension within the home, there remains a vacuum of necessary intellectual applications. With the existent intellectual cavity, the enslaved will follow their whim and cause the diet of the handler to be that of an enslaved individual.

If the handler would want to be served nourishment well-intentioned for the conscripter, they must reside amongst the enslaved realm to add the necessary intellectual ingredients. The household proceeds on the impulse of the enslaved and the occasional input of the handler. Therefore, of all the most intimate aspects of the conscripters' life, it is being tended most similar to an enslaved individual. The only way a conscripter can be tended as an absolute conscripter is if there is another conductor who oversees the household. When the handler employs managerial help, the level of production will be based on the level of intellectual development ruminating the psyche of the hired help. Whatever intellectual increases are amassed outside the household, if not integrated into the household organization, will ultimately be missing to the realm of the individual's innate realization.

Imagine the philosophers convene for a discussion about the nature of existence and return to their respective homebody. The family, workers, attendants are not privy to that learnt material, yet they interact with the philosopher in all the biological necessities. This intimacy is at a more profound level than whatever is qualified at the philosophers' roundtable. This is what transpires, for the less intimate — the most intricate conversations conversed but for the most intimate, the most menial. The spouse will engage in a role that cannot account for that knowledge yet petitions the love and pleasure of the philosopher. While comprising intellectual developments, they must perform their marital duties without equitable reciprocity. When the spouse does not reciprocate, they must reduce their intellectual standing to be on par with the others. In doing so, they have confirmed to the psyche: when appealing to a higher degree of intimacy, intellectual gains are ineffectual.

While not for Aristotle and Plato, this would be something that a pre-existing culture and a developing culture would be distressed about. They question the degree of intimacy associated with intellectual development and primarily, what is the relation to the individual. The way to measure such is to determine how thoroughly one could handle the existential chaos since it is the most intimate by its distinctive basis. When the notion of personhood contracts questions, all higher-learning and its experience becomes disremembered. One could not physiologically experience vitality to any degree while in the midst of existential dark matter. Alternatively, one could experience some sadness during a state of animation. This is because existence is formulated upon the canvas of the existential-unknown, while existential-unknown is not formulated alongside selfhood.

The pre-existing culture is self-conscious that somebody might handle the chaos better than themselves. Someone out there with an improved version to face the turmoil that can replace the pre-existing culture, sending them into the foreground of history. For if that individual, namely the developing culture arrives, the pre-existing culture would trail to the sturdier culture. In the logic that an improved version displaces pre-existing cultures from the moving pendulum of global cultural influence.

The conscripter's uneasiness is that the enslaved will overhaul them with particular ingenuity and progress. The solution that is commonly found and ironically problematic is the pre-existing culture will have them restricted; initially, as a shadow-ban to eventually an imposed ban. They cannot admit the possibility of one constructing an improved version of philosophical substance. Ironic, because the enslaved are essentially thrown into the foray of deeper existential hysteria which allows them the prospect to experience and mature it. This will allow them an advantage in confronting the experience of existential matters, if they are to retain and handle it. The weakness of the handler is that they do not reside in a level chaotic existence as do their subordinates as they maintain a certain autonomy. The enslaved, stripped of all identities and abstract deviations, in the event of a showdown, can experience the dark matter in high resolution. The disadvantage of the enslaved is that they solely reside within the narrative of the handler. This narrative seats them as unqualified for dealing with the citizen's dealings alongside obstacles that cause them to disremember and neglect their internal state.

This is the usual treatment towards developing cultures, as the usual method to suppress and inhibit is through oppression and distraction. However, while being apprehensive that the developing culture will obtain a superior culture to challenge the dark matter, they are providing that consequent culture with an unfathomable experience of that very dark matter. So each measure placed against the developing culture is in a certain sense a more advantageous position for offering the requirements to create a profound philosophy of life. The optimism on the side of the pre-existing culture is that the developing culture will lose all form of humanity and boundlessly will remain in the background. This could have been accomplished with certain underdeveloped cultures, those which do not retain a fertile embedded intellectual layer, however, in the few cases to prove to succeed, gain immeasurable ground.

Where the pre-existing culture is considered, we may say that the neglected fragments of the psyche-landscape are a result of an oversight. The pre-existing culture, regarded as profound philosophers with a promising thesis, maintains the prerogative for conducting the chaos of life with an array of intelligence and intuition. The reason for this contested feature is that the only defense against existential disarray is a broader and more comprehensive education; making sense of the senseless. The senseless individuals will capitulate at a sentiment of disarray. As the dark matter is compelling and demanding, one who has no counterclaim of animation and existence will easily betray themselves to the abyss.

We sometimes find those specimens who privilege a certain strength whilst we acknowledge a scarce psyche in position. They would be taking a particular aspect that transports a unique aspect of dark matter to platform that to the entirety of disarray. To send them to perform or experience another aspect would have them attempt the same skill which they use for everything. Such that those individuals who are presupposed to violence and are at the brink of a subsequent episode are of this kind, to which they can only handle the disarray with rather the same tool of physicality for every peculiar mode of chaos. This is to demonstrate that they can handle the chaos when they are feebler than a child to approach another aspect of the dark matter.

We may wonder as to which pathway will grant the most defense, and this increases the debate between the pre-existing culture and the developing culture. What is in agreement between them may be as important as to where they disagree. They are both advocating for the broadest education to contract as much of the dark matter as possible. This education should be amassed not by numerical value but rather, the potential in active form; of a political kind. If one were to know the intricacies of mathematics but cannot expedite such in allocating with social systems, it would be invalid of a study according to this thesis.

Therefore, both the broadness of education and its systematic implementation in a political setting is necessary. This is especially true in regard to the fundamental layer of experience. We may find one to be truly versed in a science and subsequently able to practice the study in issues that are beyond its domain. However, science can also be underdeveloped within the corporeal spaces of the psyche, so that in moments of existential doubt it may cease to exist.

Therefore, both the pre-existing culture and the developing culture appeal for the broadest and stalwart education that an individual can obtain and in doing so, can direct the chaos quite well. The difference between them is the ensuing step. The pre-existing culture assumes the role of arbitrator of all possible chaos, while the developing culture dictates that undoubtedly there is not an absolute attainment in such an arena and there will always be more stratums to deal. The solution for the developing culture is a prerequisite conjecture that their ideas are non-absolute all while still maintaining their rationality to be as advanced as possible. The pre-existing culture is not content with such a solution as it contradicts its systemic ongoings. This seemingly appears that the developing culture demands a certain duality to personhood. For the developing culture, life and death can coexist, for there is a duality that can never be solved, and the pre-existing culture desires to be continuous and transparent throughout its system.

This will always be the case, since the developing culture is representing their needs, needs which are unmet by the pre-existing culture. As such, they will be open to the vastness of understanding and merely maintain that particular themes are not adequately attended.

They are an animated role of the 'vulnerability' of the pre-existing culture, which comes to such a disappointment that they must create a new culture; that is if there would be any remaining stability to either system. However, the developing culture must give them a chance, to prove their incapability at stability, as well, the judicious claim of being held back with the continued participation of an obsolescent culture. Therefore, the duality that is present at its inception will always be in existence, thus we find that most unfaltering cultures partake in a version of duality. Moreover, if the pre-existing culture had sought its own historical root they would identify the same process.

If the pre-existing culture can demonstrate a better administration of the existential disarray, they then will have shown an accounting for all of their vulnerabilities, which with respect to this conversation is the marginalized aspects of its culture. They would require to be proficient in astuteness and knowledge to be able to operate the dark matter with aptitude. The overconfidence of the pre-existing culture would have claimed to manage it to such a degree that it may be retitled as outside the jurisdiction of dark matter; to remove the notion from the language is always a sure conveyer to a gaping vulnerability.

They are appealing to be impeccable, with only the singular shadow of their enterprise with an individual to style a more reflective prerogative on the already worn subject of their thesis. They cannot dismiss the developing culture from engaging in conversation as that would imply that they cannot mitigate contesting philosophies; they must be at footing with the contestant despite their authority and dominion. This develops to a disconcerting outcome, as they continuously assert their decaying claim without any sense of enlargement. The termination of the dialogue leaves them with a humiliated sentiment as not having a grip on their own ideas, while another has taken that dwelling of proper exploration.

The developing culture and the pre-existing culture are at odds with one another, which is a mirror representation of the superior parent-child dynamic in its political form. The superior parent, on one hand, insists on an expansive point of view which includes not only what the child contains but also the periphery that cannot be imagined by a lower-level intelligence.

The child on the other hand, asserts that the present comprehension of their perception and the specific occasion where it manifests is the only worthwhile interaction with the superior parent. The child is the rigged base that does not see more than their intrinsic situation, however, believes that such is the sole matter of affairs. The superior parent can approach the dynamic in a manner that will enable their transcendent development to partake in whatever details are committed by the child. These details are the systematic situation, as perceived by the child, to which they are sourced in a rather lineage of production which includes the superior parent, inferior parent, and society.

These details, for instance, the child's insistence on performing all superior parentsome behavior, is an absolute representation of the superior parent. Thus, they should have the right to perform their activity without the limitations of the superior parent, as they are no different. The superior parent must account for this representation within their self-derived understanding of their innate possibilities and present activity. Moreover, the superior parent retains memory traces that completely align with the child's assertions and should utilize such rapport and for being cognizant of it.

The developing culture represents the superior parent who must reengage with the pre-existing culture's material, to which they must account for their innate memory traces. This is a personal journey to the potential that may be available alongside a critical view on the present actions that may deserve attention, highlighted by the pre-existing culture.

We may want to say that the dynamic can switch, with the child representing the developing culture while the superior parent, the pre-existing culture. To which the child offers a more comprehensive, more elaborate, and more progressive approach to reality which incomes the superior parent's level of comprehension. We must understand this occasion which only takes place at a sophisticated degree of intelligence in terms of the child and thus having them accomplish what the superior parent had demanded. In this case, the superior parent must acquiesce to the children's degree of elaboration, which is analogous to the developing culture being compelled to delineate their vitality when the pre-existing culture has advanced on their position.

When such attempts, between superior parent and child, are proved to be lacking the benefits, for the superior parent in rehashing aspects of their psyche or depreciates the system to which the child ascribes, another method is to take effect. Also, we must account for the child, who may lose the reception of the superior parent and will not expand their horizon away from that committed view. To which there is a departure of each proponent from the relationship, the child continues unabated and the superior parent to other affairs. When the child has exceeded the limits unto which they represent a threat or diminished sociability, a natural urge will arise with the superior parent to reengage in the dynamic. For the departure was due to a stalemate of each failing to produce an advantages position.

However, the relationship of the superior parent to the possible nonexistence of the child, such as external threats or communal ostracization, will cause them to renew their efforts. A third reason and a common occurrence is the superior parent's apprehension for forthcoming communal dissent due to the activity of their offspring. The reengagement of the dynamic is proposed by the superior parent as to grant the child, or themselves, a socially functional and expansive situation.

Even as a stalemate accrued, it is in the likeliness of the superior parent to reenter and attempt at an advantage for themselves in the relationship. Indeed, for the functionality of the child, the superior parent is compelled to enter into their memory, potential, and current lifestyle. When the superior parent is both willing to create functionality for the child but unwilling to approach critical selfhood, certain forms of chastisement and castigation arise. This would manifest by placing the child into a functional system of dread, which would allow the superior parent to continue undeterred while the child takes a certain form of functionality.

A worse scenario manifests when the superior parent is not to protect the functionality of the child but their communal dealings to which the child is disruptive. For in this, the form of functionality for the child is not in reference to certain parameters in their innate being but rather to what the communal may perceive, not in terms of the child, but to the superior parenting aspect. An example of this is a child being dreadful in a public setting, for the superior parent takes control of the child so as to alleviate their peculiar social standing. The communal perception does not care if the child stops the unruliness due to fear of the highest degree, only that the child halts their present state. Therefore, the superior parent's dynamic with the child goes through a process in which they are in communion for certain advantages for both proponents. When those advantages diminish, the superior parent sways away from the dynamic and the child goes their naturalistic path to their inferior parent. The superior parent may reactivate that dynamic for certain concerns; both meritorious and substandard as mentioned before.

The pre-existing culture and the developing culture work in tandem in this regard, where at one point their communion to one another with its aforementioned advantages to which the conversation recedes to its eventual stalemate and each party goes their respective ways. This does not mean the dynamic is complete or has culminated only that there is a hiatus to which a further conversation will begin with either the developing or pre-existing culture seeking new advantages which rather improves their position.

State of the Victim

(The transition from a free society to servitude is relatable to any higher life form, for we are in persistent circumstances of either subjugating or in a state of subservience. We are in a position of supremacy over offspring, and one may state that any mature one in a schooling system is an authoritarian. Whilst, we are also in dynamics of subjugation, be it a dominant spouse, an organization, or neighborhood relation. The knowledge of the proper moral distinction between subservience in its morally expressive form, versus one which evolves into defeat and incessant despair, is a distinction that exemplifies an existential theme. The perspective of the pre-existing culture, the oppressor, who became normalized to the situation, claims persuasive arguments for the cause.)

The theme of victim or innocence contains another layer of complexity, one which has an evolutionary element. Bound to the evolutionary chain, higher life forms have progressed beyond their counterparts and would need to progress further without allocating for those restraints. Within the category of each of the major biological differentiations are various stages of idiosyncratic progression; within the category of apes, you would have the species of chimpanzees to contrast the orangutans. This is paralleled with higher life forms, yet the evolutionary milestones for that stage stand as intellectual and conscious capabilities. The intensification of the organism's evolution towards intellectual evolution has replaced the entire attention province of evolution.

We are even unmindful of the fact that evolution for higher life forms has shifted to the intellectual arena, by naming it intellectual development rather than intellectual evolution. This is precisely because we are manufacturing arguments from the subjective arena which is the locale for all those developments. We do not wish to remove the agency from our progression by admitting that it is being sequenced by a default environment.

After the onset of conscious and intellectual abilities, this locale was where higher life forms would permanently evolve from. The solution to all higher-life-form's evolutionary requirements, and its primary aim of reproduction, will be fast-tracked to the intellectual arena which can formulate solutions at far greater speeds than the biological process. The evolutionary purpose notwithstanding will be maintained since humans are a part of its inherent system.

Higher life forms can never formalize intellectual rhetoric to depart from the initial evolutionary purpose since it is a biological predecessor. Even the notion of self-destruction, whether on the individual level or the collective, is not a testament to this. Self-destruction is an evolutionary necessity for the occasion when higher life forms transcend their own demise and prove to be intellectually suitable. When life forms gain immortality, the mechanism that will ensure evolutionary purpose is how they make use of the possibility of inborn self-destruction.

The higher life form contains an intellectual compass that can pursue its innate development on the evolutionary chain. The mind evolves like any other organic substance, although the stipulation of the mind is that it can manipulate the chain of evolution. The mind can create tools to counter the limitations and provide expansion for the organic system, far easier than lingering for organic material to evolve for that function. Furthermore, to make use of such metabolic energy, the organic material would overhaul the mind's obligatory metabolic consumption.

Secondly, even if there is ample metabolic energy, intellectual capabilities are vital in being present for the entire biological structure. Therefore, a robust body will not maintain the availability of intellectual interests because the mind needs to attend to the body's maintenance. The feebler the body becomes, the greater the availability for the mind to transcend itself on the chain of evolution. To compensate, the mind can virtually create an infinite number of tools, even creating duplicates of itself to perform simplistic bodily functions or complex mental feats.

There is a challenging aspect of having the mind expand exponentially and correspondingly, intellectual capabilities exceeding the psyche's imagination sphere. We can perceive this overutilization within highly intelligent individuals who are deficient in social functionality. This transpires due to the vast convenience of intellectual capabilities which do not allow a correspondence with the existential nature of the organism. The biological framework in which higher life forms have extended consciousness, commences with the idea of becoming aware of selfhood. All later intellectual developments must sprout from that basic biological premise and the coinciding philosophical inquiry about its existence. When that is overshadowed, the continuing intellectual queries will lose their epicenter and become detached from societal environment. There is no evolutionary benefit for intellectual gains that are not founded on the biological system from which it originates.

Thereby, it would be an evolutionary necessity to maintain a fear response when this process is not forthcoming and more so when degenerating. This fear of reverting backward into the elementary stages of evolution would mandate continuous attention to pilot away from engagements that would cause such to occur. Due to the immense intellectual capacity of higher life forms, each individual member will retain some of those evolutionary feats. Consequently, a higher life form can progress farther than their peers through choices and intellectual pursuits. The advancement of a higher life form would expand regulation for further evolutionary progress. Analogous to multiplication, when a number is doubled, each successive stage results in a twofold increase. Within each stage of multiplication, there consists a potential that is not seeming from its appearance.

All that encompasses a year of a higher-life-form's progress during the primordial era is scalable to days of progress in the ensuing era. The contemporary era of innovation has a monthly or yearly turnover rate. We can presume that in a thousand years, innovation would entail hours instead of months, or to be genuine to the rate, seconds. The idea that colossal innovation would transpire in the span of seconds is difficult to comprehend, similar to the perceptive difficulty for an ancient mindset to reference this era's innovation. Following this pattern of thought, immortality would be achieved in the near future.

For higher life forms, competence becomes an essential component during evolution advancement. One becomes more competent the more distant they are from those inferior states of being; to be differentiated from the notion of detachment which works to the contrary. The enslaved one who loses that subsequent proficiency through coerced subjugation of their mental capacities regresses to a prior stage of evolution. Considering that no higher life form would aspire to digress towards inferior states, victimhood, especially imposed victimhood would be detestable.

This contest for competence, even as we have noted that detachment and thus parading to be a marker of incompetence, will still be seen through cultural conflict. The pre-existing culture is interested in the subjugation of the developing culture, given that they would be keen on their diminishment. This could be accomplished by placing the developing culture into a locality of victimhood, which retrogresses the higher life form to a helpless state; and thus, progression and its memory can no longer be sustained.

The mindset of the pre-existing culture is unavailable for any compromise, especially one of deliberate development for a new culture, demonstrating the true aim of the pre-existing culture. There is a personal attachment to the state of innocence which has the developing culture facilitate that embodied role. This role serves to counterpoise the lack of innocence within the pre-existing culture's systems and are nostalgic for their own "feminine" states which have been discounted; especially those which pertain to their sense of vulnerability, subtlety, and softness. These are neglected the moment a culture stagnates, and this is sought to be mirrored by whoever would be so kind as to offer such an expression. This is the reason that those who are absent from their inborn innocence may become ruthless, as they are craving more than most, a slight sense of what would constitute that, albeit through the brutal activities of their own liability.

We see parallels with an identity of a presumed agency that becomes intertwined with enslaved individuals and is eager to risk life to protect that dynamic. The incompetence of the enslaved proved the competence of the presumed agency. Furthermore, it is the only semblance of innocence and femininity that remains, almost as if their humanity is tied with the enslaved ones. They want to dispel the rising anxiety of their own regression on the evolutionary spectrum. This is done by enclosing ineffectual people as a symbol of refuting evidence.

The fact that they are exceedingly fearful proves their own incompetence. We can unmistakably see this in the lack of serious argumentation for slavery preceding the contemporary era, being that they were a peripheral culture. While the Enlightenment had deep philosophical notions about freedom, liberty, and individual rights, the opposition did not dispense with any substantial argumentation. The two primary counterarguments are economics and appreciation. The economic argument can be refuted easily; being that the presumed agency resents the competency of their drudged members which would have led to timely success.

The second argument is concerning the goodness bestowed upon the enslaved, granting them prospects they otherwise would not have had. Simple analysis would give notice to this perspective as we would never apply such rationality to everyday life. If we raised an individual's stature, we wouldn't justify any deed done upon them.

The path of healing for the enslaved might be accurately proposed as being in association with gratitude, but this distinguishes itself from the proper pathway of proficiency for the conscripter. In fact, on closer observation we can see a descent into the subjective experience of the enslaved, considering the fortune they were receiving as if it were them. Why avoid their intrinsic intellectual abilities to enjoin in the subjective necessity of gratitude within an external being. The conscripter did not consider their own moral outlook, instead, used the experience of the enslaved as a reason for their actions. *The conscripter was evolving to be the enslaved and the enslaved were being used to dispel those precise fears.*

The pre-existing culture does not like the developing culture's independence, which is a euphemism for competency. Individualism, or independence, is the mark of competence because the incompetent cannot be independent. Conflict, generally speaking, does not lead to the complete deterioration of a culture. Having a new authority take charge of a state does not deteriorate a culture, that is, unless the culture lacks sophistication from the onset.

They are not bothered about physical deterioration; the impression of replacement illustrates that the opposition is taking the role they currently maintain. This role is of intellectual competence, in which it is comical that others can take away competence from an individual treating it like a commodity. Competence is an individualistic endeavor, something that cannot be given or taken. Although education is a factor, one can seek education in any environment. Schooling is only an institutionalized form of learning and thinking. The pre-existing culture seeks to weaken the developments by making them incompetent. A society that seeks to transcend its intellectual abilities will gain tremendous progression on the evolution spectrum. The Enlightenment proved this notion by stimulating the contemporary era as we know it. The Middle Ages was a reversion to former states, and our intuition tells us such, hence the designation of being 'Dark' or 'Middle', both being disparaging terms.

Consciousness and Existential Material

There are many ways to approach conscious substance or its manifest existential material. Without a possible exploration of conscious material in a manner that will provide a continuous stream; a certain desertion is in order to proceed despite its demand. The reverence given to conscious material is an availability towards eventual integration, indebted to the notion of being imprinted upon the psyche.

A secondary approach to conscious substance is a determined position towards its radiant relevance, to revel but not approach it. Curiosity, ultimately, does not prove effective, for the mode of curiosity is to be existentially attached upon approach. When it becomes existential, we would rather phrase it as an exploration, as there is a suitable pioneer to engage in the material.

A third approach would be uncertainty towards the conscious existence, to conjecture that something dysfunctional is ascending which would eventually be found to be fraudulent. This approach appreciates that something is existent but instead of extending in the direction, would rather overstimulate additional existential demands to standstill the process. Because there is no existential answer that would prove to satisfy the entire system, this approach would prove effective. However, bypassing the conscious exploration by stating that it will see its innate decline is the same as ignoring any phenomenon, experience, or interaction, by affirming that everything declines to oblivion. This does not aid the conversation as we assume a stance in an already post-relevant period to disengage in present tendings.

A fourth approach is specific questions of conscious material. Instead of the normal method of inquiry for questions that do not contain presumed answers, this would target its vulnerabilities. Even as they appear to be accessible for conversation, when we respond to some of the gathered vulnerabilities with supplementary conscious material it will go unnoticed. This approach is both sophisticated and simplistic. Sophisticated because the individual does not permit themselves to utilize an approach that will have them free from conversation, and simplistic, because there is effort in the conversation allocated by an already ascertained conclusion. All conscious material is vulnerable by nature and to find their shadow is not a great feat.

There is another method which is prepared from a more negative disposition. This method is to find distaste in the conscious material as the bearer of the existential material. As the material is quite demanding, it can be perceived as a negative substance, all the more so when we classify individual and social failures to be owed to its existence. Once the material is assumed to be negative, it will naturally create a negative assumption of the conscious substance which brought it to bear. In this case, one would set themselves adversarial to both existential and conscious material. The conscious material can be discounted quite easily, and the existential material is utilized to vitalize that discontent. The existential demand which had arrived from conscious substance is now secondhand to be adversarial towards that consciousness; conceptual patricide.

However, even with an adversarial nature, such an individual would be found to possess a strong reverence for standing conscious substance. For they know that the interaction will create more existential material that is already reputed an outcome. Secondly, they require a certain conscious attachment to remain vital in their fight against it. If they relinquish those conscious interactions, they will become existentially uncontaminated, which even as it appears as something to pursue, they will rather have a conscious degree than no consciousness.

Existential availability is the scheme of vulnerability for which the existential self is paralleled and committed to an iota of reality. This quantity of reality is fundamentally believed as such, for which instance, a procedure within selfhood could be followed. Without that assumed reality structure, one will be unable to follow a system to interact with that component, swiftly moving from the psyche without an anchor for recurrent activity.

To place that component in the direction of recurrent activity would be to assume that somehow a form of selfhood is intertwined by way itself. This makes it possible for personhood to repeat that component, positing it to be a reality that has all perceived existence secured. Through the perspective of the unbiased observer, this component is mere scatter in the emptiness of existence. The observers' perspective is precise even as the individual undertakes a reality structure.

We cannot gain the entitlement that there is nothing of a kind as a reality structure even as it materializes that existence being no more than a vast emptiness. We must interact with that vast emptiness, which verifies that there is a juncture that presently stands on its particular area of stability for a process that tolerates interacting with that emptiness. Absolute emptiness is incapable of being interacted as it does not contain a ground of perspective for its actualization. The unbiased observer is accurate in the sense that the specific component is empty in contrast to a broader reality, indeed, every argument will be able to be contended in this fashion. We can claim that essence itself will burrow along for a much-extended period, although we do not comprise any relevance towards it; all we acknowledge will be removed from the occasion. If we remove our instance from perspective, we cannot imagine an essence and the attempt at highlighting the existential material would retain no attachment; being that we are non-existent as a point to interact with that essence.

When we pay attention to the experienced emptiness, we notice that there is an exertion of an ascending component to be a reality for at least a grasp and then to be dismissed and plummet into the background. Without that hopeful interval it would not nurse its ability. The emptiness is felt when the peak juncture of an element of perceived reality is dismissed, for it uses whatever effect that the toil had for stable ground to then bestow to an empty structure. The sense of that emptiness will be filled with the attempted reality which is declining into the vastness. Once vastness becomes the accepted state of affairs then the sense of emptiness dissipates for it has no reality to perceive that emptiness.

To illustrate this in the sequence of the day, separated by morning, afternoon, and night. The notion is that 'good' should be attributed to morning as it appears to grant a warm sentiment with its communal agreement and alignment. Then the day goes its course and depreciates, for what had appeared to be a complete reality is starting to lose its traction and the afternoon commences with a lethargic nature. Finally, the reality structure is shown to only be an act for it culminates into the backdrop of blackness with light receding. During the interval of blackness, one will find rest in the availability of creating whatever new reality they may suppose. Thus, even in that existential disarray, it can be considered a good night because it allows for the availability and capacity for an amelioration of complete personhood lost during daytime.

When we ascribe to the morning an assumed reality, personhood immediately declines with its coinciding interaction. Although the specific moment which transcends an existential state into an assumed reality structure retains the wholeness of personhood, the next instance does not. Because personhood continues its deviation or expansion, whatever is the assumed reality structure will not align with a redeploying selfhood. Eventually, the interaction with an assumed reality structure will decay in the percentile of wholesome personhood. The occurrence of respite during the night is a result of personhood becoming wholesome, albeit empty, for a new reality.

This is another way to observe an individual expressing to another "I love you," for that instance is appealed to be an interaction that partakes with the wholeness of personhood. The instance of modification from existential disarray to an assumed reality is the point of wholeness, enacted at that juncture in the timeline of that relationship. The other party is perceived as a reality structure that interacts with the wholeness of their personhood while the next instance will be absent from that wholeness.

Upon further reflection of an assumed reality structure, it becomes a grain of sand which warrants to be washed away for the greater and broader state of the entire coast. When existential availability is sought without reprieve then there is no ground-state for the individual to press an assumed reality for a cycle to take effect.

The Case for Despair of Existential Experience

There is a paradox during existential development which has been the cause of neglect of its conservation. The procedure entails a higher degree of existential material that can be wrongly ascribed as a conscious substance and reasonably a declining homestead. What doesn't aid the argument is that the definite decline would be a larger scope of existential material which goes unnoticed or unparalleled. The formula is the same and there is no way to be conscious to what we are perceiving; either the onset of a decline or a blip in progression. This will only be retroactively found out in reference to its development which can thus be concluded. To be equitable to such naysayers, all conscious substance can be perceived in hindsight as a foredawn decline. There can even be the illustration that no conscious material ever dwindles, for we cannot know the end of the universe which may reproduce from this substance.

Another portion of this paradox is that the interaction can be equivalent. While most conceptual material can be distinguished through relational factors, this is peculiar to not produce any effect of insight for a final outcome. For instance, in a situation in which two individuals are interacting, there will always be subtle material that distinguishes them. Every experience can be individuated to match specific relational content which makes it unique and capable for distinct intellectual analysis. However, the interaction with conscious substance or existential material is not convenient to be analyzed for specificity to prove to be more than its degree of material. While we could study the interaction of specific conscious material, we cannot understand its mode of consciousness apart from the degree in which it contrasts with others.

A miscalculation is made when we assume that the degree can be solely determined by conscious substance or existential material. A conscious substance without existential material may be presumed to be an elevated degree for whatever reason, however, only the existential material itself is a determinate that can be measured of varying degrees.

Another factor is practiced intimacy which has the conscious material grounded into the existential realm. Intimacy is another title for existential material that has been mediated by the biological realm. The cost of intimacy will always stimulate for more existential material, although it will burrow along to those components which will house intimacy contained by the existential realm, e.g., identity, family. The degree of intimacy will be to the effect of the existential load to be carried by the remnants. We can perceive intimacy as a method of ingesting conceptual material, nonetheless, intimacy remains a conceptualization at the nearest point on the line which divides biological and conceptual self. The appearance of the transfer through supreme levels of intimacy is only the greatest degree of its effect to make it appear as such.

Notwithstanding that in the essential realm there will never be a transfer between the two. Therefore, as fortunate as intimacy seems, it does not solve the problem and instead effectuates it to another occasion. The existential load is only nonfictional because of the transfer of consciousness. When the server has served the consumer, the transfer of intimacy appears as the interaction while the bona fide exchange is the transfer of conscious substance which brought intimacy to bear.

The existential material would always be the result of conscious substance and not standalone material. This is contrary to its appearance as a bare unknown, which we wouldn't assume to be deficient. To perceive the substance as a manifestation rather than an unknown chaos is difficult to distinguish. In the instance of how night is naturally presumed to be darkness while its more accurate interpretation is intimacy derived from prior daytime. We cannot find a novice of limited conscious and intellectual range to be also riddled with existential material. When a young adult is of this disposition, we may underestimate the conscious exposure which has been distributed their way through various means and environments.

To interact with a conscious substance which has any degree of existential material or to put it more precisely, to interact with existential material as if it contains something more appealing, is the same for either the declining substance or the progressive one. The choice of this interaction becomes paradoxical as well, for there can be no motive to interact with one formation of existential material or another. The only distinguishing factor is the degree of that material.

We can deduce without evidential reliance that for the degree of existential material is the grandiosity of the conscious or universal material. This cannot be factualized because we do not contain the exact assembly between existential and conscious material. They work together to be sure, that their facility of cohesion is aspects of conceptualized and biological material which are derivatives from higher life forms working hand in hand. The existential material is the felt experience of the biological self during an episode of disparity between conceptual formation and absolute selfhood.

Ideally, there shouldn't be any existential material as the conceptual realm should be integrated into the biological realm. Although to complete such flawlessness is nonviable because the realms are not biologically linked, at least according to biological perception. Biological perception is a vantage point which considers the biological mainframe of the organism. This perception is biologically realized but conceptually perceived. It is realized through biological connections which cannot perceive but are existent to be perceived, while the conceptual realm assists the final frame of perception. We will focus on these themes in another work.

Whatever science will be available to explain that connection, we will remain in a realm of non-actualized potential and in the process of actualization. There can never be a single entity, just as a person is distinctly required to actualize their biological potential. We will never arrive in which this is not the case, so long as there is a dynamic between potentiality and actualization.

Footnotes

[i] Haught, *Holy horrors,* 1990.

[ii] "The handler as such is concerned, not with the acquisition, but with the use of them. Yet this so-called science is not anything great or wonderful; for the handler need only know how to order that which the slave must know how to execute. Hence those who are in a position which places them above toil have stewards who attend to their households while they occupy themselves with philosophy or with politics." - Aristotle, *Politics*, bk 1, VII.

[iii] Aristotle, *Politics*, bk 1, III.

www.ingramcontent.com/pod-product-compliance
Lightning Source LLC
Chambersburg PA
CBHW070028030426
42335CB00017B/2338